Pastime **by Gerald Garston, 1984.**

"I SEE GREAT THINGS IN BASEBALL. It's our game—
the American game. It will take our people out-of-doors,
fill them with oxygen, give them a larger physical stoicism.
Tend to relieve us from being a nervous, dyspeptic set.
Repair these losses, and be a blessing to us."

—WALT WHITMAN

BASE
THE NATIONAL PASTIME

Mighty Casey
by Mark Lundeen, 1986.

BALL
IN ART AND LITERATURE

EDITED BY
DAVID COLBERT

FOREWORD BY
W. P. KINSELLA

A FAIR STREET/WELCOME BOOK

TIME
LIFE
BOOKS

CONTENTS

V. Wait Till Next Year   *Baseball fantasies*   148

VI. Knuckleballs   *The lighter side of the game*   176

VII. Glory   *The moments we live for*   203

FOREWORD

W. P. Kinsella

Cloud with hit 2 by Charles Hobson, 1990.

ANOTHER BASEBALL BOOK! What is it about baseball that enthralls the readers of America? And they are enthralled. How many books will be published about football, basketball, hockey, wrestling, or track and field? It is safe to say that there will be more books about baseball than all the others combined.

My theory as a writer is that it is the openendedness of the game that attracts both readers and writers. Consider that the other sports are twice enclosed, first by time limits, then by rigid playing boundaries. There is, of course, no time limit on a baseball game, while on a true baseball field the foul lines diverge forever eventually taking in a good part of the universe. It doesn't matter how wonderful the stars of hockey, or football, or tennis may be; they are trapped on tiny playing surfaces that make the advent of magical happenings very unlikely. On a true baseball field there is no limit to the distance that a great hitter could hit the ball, and no limit on the distance that a great outfielder could run to retrieve it. In fact, in one of my novels an outfielder runs from Iowa to New Mexico in pursuit of a fly ball. This openness makes for myth and for larger-than-life characters, two things a fiction writer hungers for. These same qualities combine to entertain the reader.

Thumbing through this book is like attending a party where all one's favorite authors are in attendance. The excerpts bring back pleasant memories. Where was I when I first read *The Universal Baseball Association, Inc.; J. Henry Waugh, Prop.*? The novel itself was a revelation and reinforcement to me, who as a young man had invented several baseball leagues like The Universal Baseball Association. When did I first encounter the lazy, sun-drenched baseball prose of Roger Angell in *The New Yorker*? The expressive writing of Angell and the simile-laden columns of Jim Murray of the *Los Angeles Times* told me, as a beginning writer, that it was all right to be poetic when describing the magical moments of baseball. I remember the thrill of first reading Bernard Malamud's *The Natural*, based partly on the legend of Shoeless Joe Jackson, and partly on the shooting of baseball star Eddie Waitkus by a deranged fan.

The other aspect that makes baseball writing so popular with both writers and readers is the dreaminess of the game. Baseball is the chess of sports, the ballet of sports. One has to be a dreamer and equipped with a fertile imagination to be a serious baseball fan. Experts tell us that in an average three-hour baseball game the ball is actually in play for less than five minutes. Those who lack imagination will quickly move on to sports fraught with constant and continuing action like basketball. In the silences of baseball the true fan reviews all the permutations and combinations that could evolve the next time the ball is put in play. If you are lucky enough to have a companion, these possibilities are discussed; and if you don't have a companion, it is often possible to speculate with total strangers, such is the intimacy of the game. There are too many possibilities to contemplate, and even with the most careful analysis the actual play is a surprise about 80 percent of the time. To the amazement of unbelievers there is never quite enough time between plays for the real fans to imagine the wondrous possibilities of what might occur next.

What editor David Colbert has collected here are little morsels of wonder; and many pieces of the world's finest baseball art are reproduced as well—colorful, humorous, breathtaking visuals. The writers represented are simply the finest ever to put pen to paper with baseball as subject matter. From the ubiquitous Stephen King, who is not thought of as a baseball writer, to Donald Hall, Pete Hamill, the irrepressible Ogden Nash, and Mark Harris, all-star baseball scribes, to amazing surprises like Lawrence Ferlinghetti, Edna Ferber, and Ishmael Reed, this compendium of poetry, fiction, nonfiction, and art will be vastly entertaining to readers whether or not they are rabid fans of the game.

—W. P. KINSELLA
October 2000

E. de K.

Edek KANSAS city BOUDREAU

INTRODUCTION
David Colbert

THIS BOOK CELEBRATES the personal experience of the game—how it feels when we play it, or watch it, or teach it.

The art and literature gathered here are presented in the way we live baseball, from childhood to old age. The book begins with our first exposure to the game—its pure joy, the warm sense of place we feel when we step on a diamond, the lessons we learn about winning and losing. It continues through our coming of age, with tests and difficulties played out on the ball field as much as anywhere. What ethical choices will we make? Are we up to the challenge? Baseball has a way of making these questions clear. Time passes, and, as every player does, we each face the difference between what we believed and what we achieved.

But just as players and fans alike are granted new hope each spring, the selections here remind us that we receive other gifts of renewal. Sometimes it's simply a second chance for an aging rookie. Sometimes it is a parent's renewed love for the game as seen through a child's eyes.

9

[OPPOSITE]
Baseball #5-A-Boudreau, Kansas City
by Elaine de Kooning, 1956.

Of course, lighter moments are also played out on the diamond. As baseball philosopher Annie Savoy said in the movie *Bull Durham*, "Baseball may be a religion full of magic, cosmic truth, and the fundamental ontological riddles of our time, but it's also a game played by men with funny socks."

Again and again, you'll encounter gifted writers and artists who return to baseball for inspiration when facing the deeper mysteries of life. Partly by choice, partly for reasons that can't be explained without references to Sigmund Freud, this childhood sport is a revered metaphor. It doesn't present its own myths, of course; we impose our old ones on it. The search for salvation in a single redeeming action, victory through moral righteousness, the need to maintain faith despite discouraging trials—we've been telling these stories forever. The title of Eliot Asinof's novel *Man on Spikes* isn't merely a reference to wearing cleats, as any reader familiar with the New Testament will recognize.

Some baseball myths, including ones in this book, are faulty. For instance, what could be more obvious and yet more wrong than the notion that baseball is an American game? David Halberstam, author of *Summer of '49* and *October 1964*, has said baseball is "the sport a foreigner is least likely to take to," to which critic David McGimpsey replies from Montreal in *Imagining Baseball*: "While Canadians, Mexicans, Nicaraguans, Guatemalans, Salvadorans, Hondurans, Costa Ricans, Panamanians, Cubans, Dominicans, Venezuelans, Filipinos, Taiwanese, Koreans, and Japanese may react negatively to the implied nationalism of such a remark, we know what Halberstam means." Believe the myths and you'll believe that racism disappeared from baseball the moment Jackie Robinson began playing for the Dodgers—and that the rest of the country has simply been trying to catch up to the pure and democratic national institution ever since. It's a nice thought, but not true. There was nothing democratic about the reserve clause, which prevented players from seeking a fair salary or moving to teams that wanted them. And the death threats sent to Hank Aaron when he neared Babe Ruth's home run record left no doubt that his skin was noticed. Nonetheless, all the fictions you will find here contain essential truths, most of them affirming the best about us.

Ultimately, every American knows that hitting a ball with a stick is sometimes about more than just hitting a ball with a stick. When a writer like Thomas Boswell says life imitates the World Series, or when Donald Hall claims baseball explains the meaning of life, nobody laughs. We all understand that baseball isn't only about baseball.

10

[OPPOSITE]
Lopez and Ump
by Elaine de Kooning, 1956.

LOPEZ

7/22/56 E deK

14

Chapter I

OPENING DAYS

First experiences of the game

"IS THERE ANYTHING THAT CAN EVOKE SPRING," novelist Thomas Wolfe once asked, "better than the sound of the ball smacking into the pocket of the big mitt, the sound of the bat as it hits the horsehide? And is there anything that can tell more about an American summer than, say, the smell of the wooden bleachers in a small-town baseball park, that resinous, sultry, and exciting smell of old dry wood?"

Wolfe may have been right, but one must wonder: With everything else there is to keep in our heads, why do our early baseball memories remain so clear? We remember every detail about our old gloves except where we last left them.

Perhaps we're wired for it. A few years ago, writer Adam Gopnik, concocting a bedtime story for his son, spun out an elaborate baseball fantasy that rivaled Scheherazade's record of 1,001 nights. It did not matter that his son had lived in France for most of his young life and knew almost nothing about baseball. He got the point and he demanded more. Can anyone explain that?

The immoderate adoration of the game, the belief that it holds the power to change our lives—these are youthful notions, but ones that neither trouble nor embarrass us. And, remarkably, one cannot foresee the children of other generations feeling differently.

Tip Top Weekly

"An ideal publication for the American Youth"

Issued weekly—By Subscription, $2.50 per year. Entered as Second Class Matter at the N. Y. Post Office by STREET & SMITH

No. 228. **Price, Five Cents.**

FRANK MERRIWELL'S SPEED

OR BREAKING THE CHICAGO COLTS

BY BURT L. STANDISH

RUNNING IN THE SAME DIRECTION AS THE BALL, THE CENTER-FIELDER, WITH OUTSTRETCHED HANDS, CAUGHT IT AS IT CAME OVER HIS SHOULDER.

"A hot dog at the ballpark is

better than steak at the Ritz."

—HUMPHREY BOGART

From
The Rookie

◆

ADAM GOPNIK

I DON'T REALLY REMEMBER how we first thought of the Rookie. I think it may have been right after I saw my then three-year-old son, Luke, playing with a soccer ball in the Luxembourg Gardens. It wasn't just the kicking that scared me but a kind of nonchalant bend-of-the-body European thing he did as he rose to meet the ball with his head. Next, he would be wearing those terrible shorts and bouncing the ball from foot to foot, improving his "skills." He had been born in New York, but he had no memory of it. Paris is the only home he knows. (Or, as he explained to a friend, in the third person he occasionally favors, like Bo Jackson or General de Gaulle, "He was born in New York, but then he moved to Paris and had a happy life.")

"You want to have a catch?" I said, and he looked at me blankly.

That night at bedtime, I said, "Hey, I'll tell you about the Rookie." It was eight o'clock, but it was bright outside. Paris is a northern city, on a latitude with Newfoundland, as New York is a Mediterranean one, on a latitude with Naples, and so the light here in the hours between seven and nine at night is like the light in the hours between five and seven in New York. The sun is still out, but the sounds have become less purposeful—you hear smaller noises, high heels on the pavement—and though it is a pleasant time to lie in bed, it is not an easy time for a small boy to go to sleep.

I had been drawing storytelling duty, for a while, and had made increasingly frantic efforts to find a hit. A story about a little boy who turned into a fish in Venice hadn't gone anywhere, and a remake of "The Hobbit" had done no box-office at all. This story, though, rolled out easily. Every dad has one good bedtime story buried in him, and desperation will bring it out.

The Rookie (I said) was a small boy in Anywhere, U.S.A., in the spring of 1908. Out walking with his mom one day, he discovered that he had an uncanny gift for throwing stones at things. He picked one up and threw it so hard that it knocked a robin off its perch a mile away; and then, after his mama chided him, he threw another one, just as far but so soft that it snuggled into the nest beside the bird without breaking an egg. His parents, a little sadly but with a sense of obligation, immediately sent him off on the train to New York, to try out for the New York Giants and their great manager, John J. McGraw. All he took with him was a suitcase that his mother had packed for him, filled with things, including his bottle, that she thought might be useful in case of an emergency. (At that point, the contents of the suitcase were unparticularized, but they eventually included a complete dictionary of the animal languages, a saxophone, a design for the first car radio, compressed early-rocketship refuelling pills, a map of Paris, a window defogger, a time machine, a Sherlock Holmes deerstalker, a map of a secret route to the South Pole, and reindeer medicine for Santa's team.)

He got out at Grand Central, took a cab all the way uptown to the Polo Grounds—his mother had told him to take taxis in New York—and asked to see John J. McGraw. McGraw, staccato and impatient, was at first skeptical, but he finally agreed to watch while the kid threw, because he was so polite and the letter from his parents was so insistent, and because, well, you never know. He called Big Six, the great Christy Mathewson, out of the dugout to watch, and Chief Meyers, the great American Indian catcher, to get behind the plate. The Chief came out, with a weary, crippled, long-suffering gait, and squatted. (I thought of the Chief as a creased veteran, though the real Chief was still in his twenties, and not yet even a Giant.) The little guy walked to the mound, tugged at his cap—not a baseball cap, the cap of his knickers suit—and let fly. Everybody was impressed, to put it mildly. "Hey, Mr. McGraw!" cried the Chief. "I ain't never seen speed like that, and ain't he got movement on it, too!" "Well," Matty said mildly, peering at the tiny, doughty figure on the mound, "when you think about it, he's more or less got to have that upward movement on his fastball, don't he?" (My

ideas of credible 1908 ballplayer dialogue were heavily influenced by Ring Lardner.) McGraw shrugged, since tryouts were one thing and baseball was another, but in the end he decided to give the kid a start that Sunday in a big benefit exhibition that the Giants were playing at the Polo Grounds against the Detroit Tigers.

I stopped. Outside, we could hear the steady, stop-and-start, rhythmic passage of the sanitation workers. Impossibly chic, in grass-green uniforms with a white stripe running down the side, the men of the Paris Propre come down our street every night to collect the garbage. The garbage is put out by *gardiens* in city-issued green plastic cannisters, and the garbagemen place the cannisters on little elevators, one on each side of the rear of the truck. The containers are lifted, turned upside down, shaken out, and returned trembling to the ground. Then the truck proceeds, at a stately, serene, implacable pace; a cabdriver who gets caught behind one on a little street lets out a moan, like a man who has just been bayonetted.

At this point, I decided I'd made a decent start and was getting ready to say good night. "Go on," he said, muffled but sharp, from under his covers. An order.

In the benefit exhibition that Sunday (I went on at last), the big bathtub-shaped stadium, with its strange supporting Y beams, was packed with fans, come to see the three-year-old phenom. The Rookie took the mound, throwing smoke, and it looked as though it might be a first, a perfect perfect game, twenty-seven men up, twenty-seven K's, until, in the sixth, he had to face the Terrible Ty Cobb. (I realized that I had a problem here, since Cobb should have been batting cleanup from the start; I explained that he had been late suiting up, because he insisted on extorting extra payment from the Tigers management for playing in a charity exhibition, even though everybody else was playing for free. Cobb was just like that, I explained: terrible.) The crowd quieted as the confrontation neared. Cobb came to the plate, sneering and drawling.

"Hey, baby," he called out, taunting the Rookie. "Looks to me like you're nothing but a *baby*." (Luke's whole body stiffened; if there was a worse insult, he hadn't heard it—Jackie Robinson, in his first year with the Brooklyn Dodgers, had never been called a name so vile.) Shaken, the Rookie lost a bit off his heater. It was still blazing, though, and Cobb just got a piece of it, dribbling it toward first, he took off, and the Rookie, who knew his assignments, dutifully scampered over to cover. Cobb came in hard, hard as he could, his spikes sharpened to razor tips, and stamped down on the Rookie's three-year-old foot. The Rookie dropped the ball. Safe! Stinking rotten way to get on base, but safe all the same. Shaking off a couple of tears, the Rookie went back to the mound. "Hey, I reckon you're a crybaby. Hey, everybody—look at the crybaby! Looks to me like you're nothin' but a crybaby" came the taunting Georgia drawl from first, and the Rookie pitched out of trouble. But the pain lingered, and, in the top of the ninth, the Giants having pushed over one run on a hit-and-run executed by the Chief, he made a few mistakes, walked a couple of batters—hey, he was three—and left himself with the bases loaded and the Georgia Peach due up again. The crowd was going crazy, and now the taunting began again, worse than ever. ("Hey, baby! Hey, crybaby! Whyn't ya cry some more, crybaby?")

The Rookie knew what he had to do. In the dugout, he had taken his old bottle from the suitcase his mother had packed for him when he went off to join the Giants, just in case, and stowed it under his cap. Now he dripped a couple of drops of milk onto the seams of the baseball— the Rookie's soon-to-be notorious bottleball. It was before they brought in the rule against foreign substances on the ball, I explained. The Rookie was playing fair.

("Hey, when are you guys going to sleep" Luke's mother's voice came from the other room. "Soon," I called back abruptly. The lights of the traffic on the Boulevard Saint-Germain came in

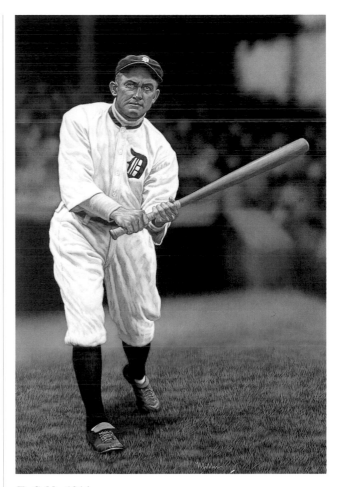

Ty Cobb, 1914
by Arthur K. Miller, 1996.

21

through the windows, but I didn't even draw the curtains.)

The Rookie stretched and threw, and the bottleball dipped and twisted and dipped and twisted again—curving all the way out to the third-base line and then cruising halfway toward first before finally slipping in, soft and clean, right across the plate, a strike at the knees. Cobb had time to take a really good cut—he had *all day*—but the pitch had him so fooled that he didn't just whiff, he twisted himself in knots while he whiffed: real knots, his whole body pulled around like a wet washrag, hands ending up back of his butt. (Luke chuckled deeply at that.) "Steer-rike-uh three" cried the Umpire. The bleachers of the Polo Grounds went nuts.

The Rookie trotted off the field. "Who's the baby now, Mr. Cobb?" he asked, with quiet dignity, on his way back to the dugout.

My kid sat up, shot up in bed, like a mechanical doll, as though he had a spring hinge right at his waist. Christy Mathewson (I went on) didn't say anything—that wasn't his way—but he went over as the Rookie came into the dugout, took off the Rookie's cap, and mussed up his hair. Outside, the crowd wouldn't leave. They chanted "Rookie! Rookie!"

Now the only sound from Luke's pillow was of short, constant breathing. I had the uncanny knowledge of a kind of silent excitement, the certainty—I have witnessed it once or twice on opening night in a theatre, though I had certainly never created it before myself—that what we had here was a hit. The Terrible Ty Cobb had called him a baby and he had thrown the bottleball, and then who was the baby?

That night (I said), the Rookie was offered a contract with the Giants (doubtless a mean, exploitative contract, but I left that out), and the team got on the overnight sleeper to St. Louis, heading out to steamy Sportsman's Park. (I knew that the Browns played there, not the Cardinals, but I liked the way it sounded.) The Chief tucked the Rookie into his berth and, before he went off to play pinochle with the guys, asked him, gruffly,

Christy Mathewson
by Arthur K. Miller, 1993.

"You O.K., Rookie?" "I'm O.K., Chief," the Rookie said, and then he listened to the sounds of the train tracks clacking and the whistle blowing and the other ballplayers in the next car, laughing and playing cards, before he fell deep asleep, somewhere outside Columbus.

"I'm O.K., Chief," Luke repeated, and he did something he had never done before, or, at least, not in my presence: without negotiation or hesitation, without tears or arguments or requests to come and sleep in the big bed, he rolled right over and fell asleep.

◆　◆　◆

FROM THEN ON, we had a story about the Rookie—Luke called it "the Rookie story"—every night. The characters firmed up pretty quickly. The Rookie was an earnest, resourceful, somewhat high-strung little hero. The Chief was blustery and honest, wanting nothing more than to settle in with his copy of the *Police Gazette* and have a peaceful afternoon at McSorley's. The Rookie's triumph over Ty Cobb, though, had bad consequences. Cobb developed a bitter, unappeasable Tom DeLay-type enmity toward the Rookie, and set himself the task of doing anything he could to destroy his career. John J. McGraw, thumbtack-sharp and demanding, and Christy Mathewson, handsome and deep-voiced and friendly, though a little remote—on a couple of occasions, when the Chief left town to go on a scouting trip to Cincinnati, he was the Rookie's babysitter—filled out the dramatis personae.

After a couple of months, I went down to the cellar of our building and got out the few baseball reference books I had brought to Paris and never unpacked. (This cellar is an honest-to-god *cave*, a stone cellar with little arches where you could keep wine; I kept meaning to bring the wine down, but I never remembered to do it, and, instead, the books were there, moldering away.) The 1908 National League pennant race, which I had plucked out of the air and dim memories of "The Glory of Their Times," turned

out to be even more interesting than I'd thought. It was a three-way race—Cubs, Giants, Pirates—that included Merkle's boner and the season-capping rematch it produced, and, in a sense, it made baseball in America. I discovered that 1908 had been a kind of watershed year, a time when baseball had, for the last time, an air of improvisation about it, with, as someone said of those days, "stupid guys, smart guys, tough guys, mild guys, crazy guys, college men, slickers from the city, and hicks from the country." If a three-year-old with a major-league fastball had ever existed, 1908 would have been the right season for him to play, and they probably would have roomed him with an American Indian catcher.

I even found a wonderful photograph of the Polo Grounds in that magical year, and we hung it over Luke's bed. It shows a hundred or so fans lining up on Coogan's Bluff, overlooking the ballpark—too poor or, more likely, too cheap to buy tickets, since you can see that there are still a few seats left in center—backs turned and heads bowed as they stare down at the field. Every single one of the men (there are no women) is wearing a derby; the kids are wearing cloth caps. One kid and an elderly gent have got up on a barrel, and five men in suits and hats are standing, precarious but dignified, on a plank that slopes down from it. You can't really see a thing going on in the park—not a base line, not a ballplayer, not a glimpse of a dugout or a bullpen, nothing except the outfield grass down below, a perfect and absolute blank. It's as good as a Magritte: the solemnly dressed businessmen, backs turned, gazing out at the bare and uneventful field. Of course, Luke didn't have to be told who they were looking at down there, and why; we could both see it plain as day. They were watching the Rookie, pitching his way out of another pinch. ❖

[FOLLOWING PAGES]
The American National Game of Base Ball: Grand Match for the Championship at the Elysian Fields, Hoboken, N.J. by Currier and Ives, 1866.

23

[OPPOSITE]
The Saturday Evening Post **cover**
by John Clymer, April 21, 1951.

From
An American Childhood

◆

ANNIE DILLARD

ON THE YELLOW BACK WALL of our Richland Lane garage, I drew a target in red crayon. The target was a batter's strike zone. The old garage was dark inside; I turned on the bare bulb. Then I walked that famously lonely walk out to the mound, our graveled driveway, and pitched.

I squinted at the strike zone, ignoring the jeers of the batter—oddly, Ralph Kiner. I received no impressions save those inside the long aerial corridor that led to the target. I threw a red-and-blue rubber ball, one of those with a central yellow band. I wound up; I drew back. The target held my eyes. The target set me spinning as the sun from a distance winds the helpless spheres. Entranced and drawn, I swung through the moves and woke up with the ball gone. It felt as if I'd gathered my own body, pointed it carefully, and thrown it down a tunnel bored by my eyes.

I pitched in a blind fever of concentration. I pitched, as I did most things, in order to concentrate. Why do elephants drink? To forget. I loved living at my own edge, as an explorer on a ship presses to the ocean's rim; mind and skin were one joined force curved out and alert, prow and telescope. I pitched, as I did most things, in a rapture.

Now here's the pitch. I followed the ball as if it had been my own head, and watched it hit the painted plastered wall. High and outside; ball one. While I stood still stupefied by the effort of the pitch, while I stood agog, unbreathing, mystical, and unaware, here came the doggone rubber ball again, bouncing out of the garage.

And I had to hustle up some snappy fielding, or lose the ball in a downhill thicket next door.

The red, blue, and yellow ball came spinning out to the driveway, and sprang awry on the gravel; if I nabbed it, it was apt to bounce out of my mitt. Sometimes I threw the fielded grounder to first—sidearm—back to the crayon target, which had become the first baseman. Fine, but the moronic first baseman spat it back out again at once, out of the dark garage and bouncing crazed on the gravel; I bolted after it, panting. The pace of this game was always out of control.

So I held the ball now, and waited, and breathed, and fixed on the target till it mesmerized me into motion. In there, strike one. Low, ball two.

Four balls, and they had a man on. Three strikeouts, and you had retired the side. Happily, the opposing batters, apparently paralyzed by admiration, never swung at a good pitch. Unfortunately, though, you had to keep facing them; the retired side resurrected immediately from its ashes, fresh and vigorous, while you grew delirious—nutsy, that is, from fielding a bouncing ball every other second and then stilling your heart and blinking the blood from your eyes so you could concentrate on the pitch.

◆ ◆ ◆

AMY'S FRIEND TIBBY had an older brother, named Ricky; he was younger than I was, but available. We had no laughing friendship, such as I enjoyed with Pin Ford, but instead a working relationship: we played a two-handed baseball game. Tibby and Ricky's family lived secluded at the high dead end of Richland Lane. Their backyard comprised several kempt and gardened acres. It was here in the sweet mown grass, here between the fruit trees and the rhubarb patch, that we passed long, hot afternoons pitching a baseball. Ricky was a sober, good-looking boy, very dark; his father was a surgeon.

We each pitched nine innings. The other caught, hunkered down, and called each pitch a ball or a strike. That was the essence of it: Catcher called it. Four walks scored a side. Three outs retired a side, and the catcher's side came on to pitch.

This was practically the majors. You had a team to root for, a team that both received pitches and dished them out. You kept score. The pitched ball came back right to you—after a proper, rhythmical interval. You had a real squatting catcher. Best, you had a baseball.

The game required the accuracy I was always working on. It also required honor. If when you were catching you made some iffy calls, you would be sorry when it was your turn to pitch. Ricky and I were, in this primitive sense, honorable. The tag ends of summer— before or after camp, before or after Lake Erie—had thrown us together for this one activity, this chance to do some pitching. We shared a catcher's mitt every inning; we pitched at the catcher's mitt. I threw as always by imagining my whole body hurled into the target; the rest followed naturally. I had one pitch, a fast ball. I couldn't control the curve. When the game was over, we often played another. Then we thanked each other formally, drank some hot water from a garden hose, and parted—like, perhaps, boys.

◆　◆　◆

ON TUESDAY SUMMER evenings I rode my bike a mile down Braddock Avenue to a park

where I watched Little League teams play ball. Little League teams did not accept girls, a ruling I looked into for several years in succession. I parked my bike and hung outside the chain-link fence and watched and rooted and got mad and hollered, "Idiot, catch the ball!" "Play's at first!" Maybe some coach would say, "Okay, sweetheart, if you know it all, you go in there." I thought of disguising myself. None of this was funny. I simply wanted to play the game earnestly, on a diamond, until it was over, with eighteen players who knew what they were doing, and an umpire. My parents were sympathetic, if amused, and not eager to make an issue of it.

At school we played softball. No bunting, no stealing. I had settled on second base, a spot Bill Mazeroski would later sanctify: lots of action, lots of talk, and especially a chance to turn the double play. Dumb softball: so much better than no ball at all, I reluctantly grew to love it. As I got older, and the prospect of having anything to do with young Ricky up the street became out of the question, I had to remind myself, with all loyalty and nostalgia, how a baseball, a real baseball, felt.

A baseball weighted your hand just so, and fit it. Its red stitches, its good leather and hardness like skin over bone, seemed to call forth a skill both easy and precise. On the catch—the grounder, the fly, the line drive—you could snag a baseball in your mitt, where it stayed, snap, like a mouse locked in its trap, not like some pumpkin of a softball you merely halted, with a terrible sound like a splat. You could curl your fingers around a baseball, and throw it in a straight line. When you hit it with a bat it cracked—and your heart cracked, too, at the sound. It took a grass stain nicely, stayed round, smelled good, and lived lashed in your mitt all winter, hibernating. ❖

Isabelle Alvarez by **Lance Richbourg, 1994.**

Instruction

◆

CONRAD HILBERRY

The coach has taught her how to swing,
run bases, slide, how to throw
to second, flip off her mask for fouls.

Now, on her own, she studies
how to knock the dirt out of her cleats,
hitch up her pants, miss her shoulder
with a stream of spit, bump
her fist into her catcher's mitt,
and stare incredulously at the ump.

From
The Girl Who Loved Tom Gordon

◆

STEPHEN KING

SITTING ON HER TREE-TRUNK, Trisha laughed and clapped her hands and then resettled her signed Tom Gordon hat more firmly on her head. It was full dark now.

In the bottom of the eighth, Nomar Garciaparra hit a two-run shot into the screen on top of the Green Monster. The Red Sox took a five-to-four lead and Tom Gordon came on to pitch the top of the ninth.

Trisha slid off the fallen tree to the ground. The bark scraped against the wasp-stings on her hip, but she hardly noticed. Mosquitoes settled with immediate hungry intent on her bare back where her shirt and the tatters of the blue poncho had rucked up, but she didn't feel them. She gazed at the last held glimmerglow in the brook—fading tarnished quicksilver—and sat on the damp ground with her fingers pressed to the sides of her mouth. Suddenly it seemed very important that Tom Gordon should preserve the one-run lead, that he should secure this victory against the mighty Yankees, who had lost a pair to Anaheim at the start of the season and had hardly lost since.

"Come on, Tom," she whispered. In a Castle View hotel room her mother was in an agony of terror; her father was on a Delta flight from Boston to Portland to join Quilla and his son; at the Castle County state police barracks, which had been designated Rally Point Patricia, search-parties very much like the ones the lost girl had imagined were coming back in after their first fruitless sallies; outside the barracks, newsvans from three TV stations in Portland and two in Portsmouth were parked; three dozen experienced woodsmen (and some *were* accompanied by dogs) remained in the forests of Motton and the three unincorporated townships which stretched off toward New Hampshire's chimney: TR-90, TR-100, and TR-110. The consensus among those remaining in the woods was that Patricia McFarland must still be in Motton or TR-90. She was a little girl, after all, and likely hadn't wandered far from where she had last been seen. These experienced guides, game wardens, and Forest Service men would have been stunned to know that Trisha had gotten almost nine miles west of the area the searchers considered their highest priority.

"Come on, Tom," she whispered. "Come on, Tom, one two three, now. You know how it goes."

But not tonight. Gordon opened the top of the ninth by walking the handsome yet evil Yankee shortstop, Derek Jeter, and Trisha remembered something her father had once told her: when a team gets a lead-off walk, their chances of scoring rise by seventy percent.

If we win, if Tom gets the save, I'll *be saved.* This thought came to her suddenly—it was like a firework bursting in her head.

It was stupid, of course, as dopey as her father knocking on wood before a three-and-two pitch (which he did every time), but as the dark drew deeper and the brook gave up its final silver tarnish, it also seemed irrefutable, as obvious as two-and-two-makes-four: if Tom Gordon got the save, *she* would get the save.

Paul O'Neill popped up. One out. Bernie Williams came up. "Always a dangerous hitter," Joe Castiglione remarked, and Williams immediately ripped a single to center, sending Jeter to third.

"*Why* did you say that, Joe?" Trisha moaned. "Oh cripes, why did you have to *say* that?"

Runners on first and third, only one out. The Fenway crowd cheering, hoping. Trisha could imagine them leaning forward in their seats.

"Come on, Tom, come *on*, Tom," she whispered. The cloud of minges and noseeums were still all around her, but she no longer noticed. A feeling of despair touched her heart, cool and strong—it was like that hateful voice she had discovered in the middle of her head. The Yankees were too good. A base hit would tie it, a long ball would put it out of reach, and the awful, *awful* Tino Martinez was up, with the most dangerous hitter of all right behind him; the Straw Man would now be down on one knee in the on-deck circle, swinging a bat and watching.

Gordon worked the count on Martinez to two and two, then threw his curveball. "*Struck him out!*" Joe Castiglione shouted. It was as if he couldn't believe it. "Aw, man, that was a beauty! Martinez must have missed it by a foot!"

"*Two* feet," Troop added helpfully.

"So it all comes to this," Joe said, and behind his voice Trisha could hear the volume of the other voices, the fan voices, begin to rise. The rhythmic clapping started. The Fenway Faithful were getting to their feet like a church congregation about to sing a hymn. "Two on, two out, Red Sox clinging to a one-run lead, Tom Gordon on the mound, and—"

"Don't you say it," Trisha whispered, her hands still pressing against the sides of her mouth, "don't you *dare* say it!"

But he did. "And the always dangerous Darryl Strawberry coming to the plate."

That was it; game over; great Satan Joe Castiglione had opened his mouth and jinxed it. Why couldn't he just have given Strawberry's *name*? Why did he have to start in with that "always dangerous" horsepucky when any fool knew that only *made* them dangerous?

"All right, everybody, fasten your seat belts," Joe said. "Strawberry cocks the bat. Jeter's dancing around third, trying to draw a throw or at least some attention from Gordon. He gets neither. Gordon looks in. Veritek flashes the sign. To the set. Gordon throws . . . *Strawberry swings and misses*, strike one. Strawberry shakes his head as if he's disgusted . . . "

"Shouldn't be disgusted, that was a pretty good pitch," Troop remarked, and Trisha, sitting in the dark bugblown armpit of nowhere, thought, *Shut up, Troop, just shut up for a minute.*

"Straw steps out . . . taps his cleats . . . now he's back in. Gordon with the look to Williams on first . . . to the set . . . he pitches. *Out*side and low."

Trisha moaned. The tips of her fingers were now so deeply pressed into her cheeks that her lips were pulled up in a strange distraught smile. Her heart was hammering in her chest.

"Here we go again," Joe said. "Gordon's ready. He fires, Strawberry swings, *and it's a long high drive to right field, if it stays fair it's gone, but it's drifting . . . it's drifting . . . drifffffting . . .*"

Trisha waited, breath caught.

"Foul," Joe said at last, and she began to breathe again. "But that was toooo close. Strawberry just missed a three-run homer. It went on the wrong side of the Pesky Pole by no more than six or eight feet."

"I'd say four feet," Troop added helpfully.

"I'd say you've got *stinky* feet," Trisha whispered. "Come on, Tom, come on, *please*." But he wouldn't; she knew that now for sure. Just this close and no closer.

Still, she could see him. Not all tall and ginky-looking like Randy Johnson, not all short and tubby-looking like Rich Garces. Medium height, trim . . . and handsome. *Very* handsome, especially with his cap on, shading his eyes . . . except her father said almost all ballplayers were handsome. "It comes with the genes," he told her, then added: "Of course a lot of them have nothing upstairs, so it all balances out." But Tom Gordon's looks weren't the thing. It was the stillness before he pitched which had first caught her eye and her admiration. He didn't stalk around the mound like some of them did, or bend to fiddle with his shoes, or pick up the rosin bag and then toss it back down in a little flump of white dust. No, Number 36 simply waited for the batter to finish all of *his* fiddle-de-diddling. He was so still in his bright white uniform as he waited for the batter to be ready. And then, of course, there was the thing he did whenever he succeeded in getting the save. That thing as he left the mound. She loved that.

"Gordon winds and fires . . . and it's in the dirt! Veritek blocked it with his body and that saved a run. The *tying* run."

"Stone the crows!" Troop said.

Joe didn't even try to dignify that one. "Gordon takes a deep breath out on the mound. Strawberry stands in. Gordon wheels . . . deals . . . *high*."

A storm of booing rose in Trisha's ears like an ill wind.

"Thirty thousand or so umps in the stands didn't agree with that one, Joe," Troop remarked.

"True, but Larry Barnett behind the plate's got the final say and Barnett said it was high. The count runs full to Darryl Strawberry. Three and two."

In the background the rhythmic clapping of the fans swelled. Their voices filled the air, filled her head. She knocked on the wood of the tree-trunk without realizing she was doing it.

"The crowd's on its feet," Joe Castiglione said, "all thirty thousand of them, because no one has left the joint tonight."

"Maybe one or two," Troop said. Trisha took no notice. Neither did Joe.

"Gordon to the belt."

Yes, she could see him at the belt, hands together now, no longer facing home plate directly but looking in over his left shoulder.

"Gordon into the motion."

She could see this, too: the left foot coming back toward the planting right foot as the hands—one wearing the glove, one holding the ball—rose to the sternum; she could even see Bernie Williams, off with the pitch, streaking for second, but Tom Gordon took no notice and even in motion his essential stillness remained, his eyes on Jason Veritek's mitt, hung behind the plate low and toward the outside corner.

"Gordon delivers *the three . . . two . . . pitch AND*—"

The crowd told her, the sudden joyous thunder of the crowd.

"*Strike three called!*" Joe was nearly screaming. "*Oh my goodness, he threw the curve on three and two and froze Strawberry! The Red Sox win five to four over the Yankees and Tom Gordon gets his eighteenth save!*" His voice dropped into a more normal register. "Gordon's teammates head for the mound with Mo Vaughn pumping his fist in the air and leading the charge, but before Vaughn gets there, it's Gordon with the quick gesture, the one the fans have gotten to know very well in just the short time he's been the Sox closer."

Trisha burst into tears. She pushed the power button on the Walkman and then just sat there on the damp ground with her back against the tree-trunk and her legs spread and the blue poncho hanging between them in its hula-skirt tatters. She cried harder than she had since first realizing for sure that she was lost, but this time she cried in relief. She was lost but would be found. She was sure of it. Tom Gordon had gotten the save and so would she. ❖

33

The Perfect American Place

◆

LESLEY HAZLETON

IT WAS A SUNNY, DRY SEPTEMBER SUNDAY—the kind of day that can convince an unsuspecting stranger that New York is a wonderful place to spend the summer. I was fresh off the plane from Israel. It was only my second day in the United States, but my friends here had made the shocked discovery that I had never even seen a baseball diamond. So they took me out to the ball game. Thurman Munson had been killed in a plane crash a few weeks before, and the Yankees weren't going to be in any World Series that year. But this particular Sunday had been declared Catfish Hunter day. Ole Catfish was retiring, and New York had turned out for him.

Maybe it was in comparison with the parched browns of Israel at summer's end. Maybe it was the combined smell of hot dogs and marijuana drifting over the stands. Maybe it was the light. All I know for sure is that when I emerged from the tunnel and stood there in the first tier, looking out over home base, I gasped at the perfect greenness of it. So this was a diamond.

What happened then was everything I expected from America. A brass band, heavy on the epaulets and the drums. High-stepping marching girls in white rubber bootees and pompons, throwing silver plywood rifles twisting into the air. A whole ceremony right on the field, including Catfish's mother, wife and two young boys, and of course Catfish himself—the archetype of the huntin'-shootin'-fishin' man. Speeches were made and messages read. Gifts were hauled, driven and led out onto the field (television sets, Toyota cars and a live elephant, respectively). And then came a hush as Catfish approached the microphone.

"There's three men shoulda been here today," he said. "One's my pa"—riotous applause—"one's the scout that signed me"—more riotous applause—"and the third one"—pause—"is Thurman Munson." Riot. Fifty thousand people up on their feet and roaring, including my friends. The fifty thousand and first—myself—looked on in bewilderment. I missed Catfish's next sentence, but I'll never forget the last one of that brief speech. "Thank you, God," he said, "for giving me strength, and making me a ballplayer."

And suddenly I too was up on my feet and cheering. It was the perfect American day, the perfect American place, the perfect American sentence. That combination of faith and morality, sincerity and naiveté, was everything my Old-World preconceptions had led me to expect, and as I watched Catfish walk off the field into the sunset of the Baseball Hall of Fame, leading his little boy with one hand and the elephant with the other, I felt that I had had my first glimpse of a mythical place called America. ❖

Old Yankee Stadium. The First Night Game, May 28, 1946 by Paolo Corvino, 1969.
The Museum of the City of New York.

The Grip of the Game

◆

THOMAS BOSWELL

FRIENDS HAVE DECIDED TO GIVE our new son every variety of baseball paraphernalia known to the baby industry. He has a tiny warmup jacket (in case it's blustery as he crawls in from the bullpen). He has his choice of uniform. If anybody tried to throw an almost weightless Styrofoam ball past him, he has an almost weightless Styrofoam bat with which to hit it. That is, unless he wants to catch it with his equally weightless glove. Needless to say, he has hats and even a batting helmet with an earflap.

As you can see, there's an excellent chance that Russell Boswell, assuming he has a shred of independence in his nature, will grow up to hate baseball. This would, no doubt, be a fitting piece of poetic justice for his father, who has prolonged his own infancy well beyond the normal limit with the aid of this particular game. However, it would be a shame for the little boy.

Baseball was meant, and still is meant, to be irresponsible, anti-adult, silly, lyric, inexplicable, slightly rebellious and generally disreputable. The ballpark is the place you go to play hooky. When you get there, you scream, yell insults at grown millionaires, knock people aside chasing foul balls and eat nachos until your stomach is so full that you have to switch to ice cream sandwiches.

Edwin Pope, who writes a sports column for the *Miami Herald*, recalls that when he took his six-year-old boy to his first pro game, the lad said, "Where do I throw the peanut shells, dad?" To which Pope, with great delight, said, "On the floor, son."

That's baseball. Peanut shells on the floor. As much noise as you can make. And who knows what sort of person might sit next to you and yell what outrageous thing. Once, a quarter-century ago, I heard a man at RFK Stadium vow that he would swallow an entire sports section if Frank Howard ("Hondo, my hero—you big bum," he yelled over and over for two hours) hit a home run. Howard did, and the man spent the rest of the game slowly tearing the paper into strips and eating them.

They call baseball the summer game, which, to a child, means vacation and laziness and multifarious mischief. When you're indoctrinated from the cradle that baseball is officially acceptable, what chance have you got? My plan is to start piano lessons early and forbid the throwing of any ball within a hundred yards of home. That should set Russell on the noble track of showing his old man that he'll do just what he wants to do.

In *Ball Four*, Jim Bouton said he'd spent his life gripping a baseball and only after he retired did he come to realize it'd been the other way around. Baseball has more grips than Eddie Murray has stances and, whichever way you turn, the game grabs you in a different place. However, one of its most basic but least-mentioned holds is that it's obviously a bunch of foolishness from first to last. The more we belabor serious "issues" in the game, the more the small child in us wants to laugh and run down an upper-deck aisle, imperiling soft drink vendors. For summer fun in my formative years, two friends and I would climb to the top row at RFK with a hand-cranked siren and wind it up to such a crescendo that the crowd (usually 3,751) snickered and the rent-a-cops came running to apprehend us.

As well as being many other things, baseball is a wonderful waste of time, a raspberry in the face of authority. The same long division that plagues the grade schooler becomes a joy when it's his hero's batting average that's being computed. Arithmetic in pursuit of grades can be done hurriedly on the bus to school. Math for the sake of a batting title must be completed before breakfast and double-checked.

One promise of Opening Day is that every day for the next seven months the possibility of reckless, feckless escape is as close as the TV button, the radio switch, the morning newspaper, the weekly *Sporting News* or a trip to the park. There's baseball, waiting to burn our time as though we'd never age and tempt us to care deeply about a thing so obviously trivial that, minutes after the last pitch, we're laughing in our beer and knocking the manager.

Even our baseball sorrow is a delicious fakery. Ah, those poor Red Sox fans. To break good china in true rage, like one loyal Boston fan I know, then have to answer the phone and know it's a friend calling to mock your misery—yes, that's carefree, wait-till-next-year, better-to-have-loved-and-lost bonding that baseball fans share.

It is with some sorrow that we note the advent of respectability in the game. When men like Peter Ueberroth and A. Bartlett Giamatti set up shop atop a sport, as a suitable career stop between this presidency and that, it causes anxiety; why can't we have lovable Happy Chandler or befuddled Bowie Kuhn? These days, lawyers run Rotisserie League teams and "sabermetricians" cross swords with 500-page tomes, debating the exegesis of comically obscure stats. How can the game be dragged back to the state of ramshackle disrepute where it belongs, thrives and merits the love of children?

Much of the spirit of baseball lies with anarchic men like Bill Veeck, who would send a midget up to bat, give away a wheelbarrow of money, blow up a scoreboard or say that Kuhn was stiff-necked because he never got over being named after a racetrack.

The great men of baseball, though we don't say it too often, tend to eat hot dogs until they are hospitalized or discuss traffic violations with police while kicking in the cruiser door. When we scratch the surface of our Ruths, Roses, Weavers and Jacksons, we find appetite and

laughter and a wayward nonchalance that would be self-destructive in the lives of most of us.

In short, baseball is brave and scatterdash enough to fascinate a child and fit comfortably among such favorite pursuits as (let's see if I remember) climbing a condemned water tower or exploring a haunted old (Revolutionary War) fort. Those of us who are guilty of scrubbing baseball behind the ears and making it appear a mite more upstanding than it ever could be should apologize and promise not to sin again. For at least a day. ❖

Man on Second
by Leonard Dufresne, 1975.

38

From
A Personal History
of the Curveball

◆

JONATHAN HOLDEN

After school, not knowing
what to look for, only
that we'd know it when it came —
that it would be strange —
we'd practice curves, trying
through trial and error to pick up by luck
whatever secret knack a curveball took,
sighting down the trajectory
of each pitch we caught
for signs of magic.
Those throws spun in like drills
and just as straight,
every one the same.

Chapter II

IN PLAY

HERE ARE THE PEOPLE, places, and things of baseball: stars whose statistics are memorized; big-day excitement in a small-town ballpark; a sandlot player's obsessive affection for a bat or glove; the creeping tension of a runner about to steal second.

The pieces that follow recall timeless moments: Bob Greene rhapsodizes about the Louisville Slugger; Edna Ferber captures the unique charms of bush-league baseball. A little history is here, too: William Hooper describes the culture of the game circa 1871; Albert Spalding traces the development of the game into this century.

Throughout, one is reminded that the game's essence is joy. "There is really nothing in life," novelist Philip Roth once wrote, "nothing at all, that quite compares with that pleasure of rounding second base at a nice slow clip, because there's just no hurry any more, because that ball you've hit has just gone sailing out of sight."

Before all the profound thoughts about the national pastime comes the pastime itself. So here is the heart of the literary order—not the metaphysical or the eccentric. Just the game, as we play it.

Baseball people, places, and things

"Trying to sneak a pitch past Hank Aaron is like trying to sneak the sunrise past a rooster."

—JOE ADCOCK

Hammerin' Hank Aaron by **Brinah Bank Kessler, 1993.**

Yankee Stadium Diptych **by Joseph Golinkin, 1989.**

Take Me Out
to the Ball Game

◆

LYRICS BY JACK NORWORTH,
MUSIC BY ALBERT VON TILZER

Katie Casey was baseball mad
Had the fever and had it bad
Just to root for the home town crew
Every sou Katie blew
On a Saturday her young beau
Called to see if she'd like to go
To see a show, but Miss Kate said, "No
I'll tell you what you can do."

Take me out to the ball game
Take me out with the crowd
Buy me some peanuts and Cracker Jack
I don't care if I never get back
Let me root, root, root for the home team
If they don't win, it's a shame
For it's one, two, three strikes, you're out
At the old ball game

Katie Casey saw all the games
Knew the players by their first names
Told the umpire he was wrong
All along, good and strong
When the score was just two to two
Katie Casey knew what to do
Just to cheer up the boys she knew
She made the gang sing this song

Line-up for Yesterday:
An ABC of Baseball Immortals

◆

OGDEN NASH

A is for Alex
The great Alexander;
More goose eggs he pitched
Than a popular gander.

B is for Bresnahan
Back of the plate;
The Cubs were his love,
And McGraw was his hate.

C is for Cobb,
Who grew spikes and not corn,
And made all the basemen
Wish they weren't born.

D is for Dean.
The grammatical Diz,
When they asked, Who's the tops?
Said correctly, I is.

E is for Evers,
His jaw in advance;
Never afraid
To Tinker with Chance.

F is for Fordham
And Frankie and Frisch
I wish he were back
With the Giants, I wish.

G is for Gehrig,
The Pride of the Stadium;
His record pure gold,
His courage, pure radium.

H is for Hornsby;
When pitching to Rog,
The pitcher would pitch,
Then the pitcher would dodge.

I is for Me,
Not a hard-sitting man,
But an outstanding all-time
Incurable fan.

J is for Johnson
The Big Train in his prime
Was so fast he could throw
Three strikes at a time.

K is for Keeler,
As fresh as green paint,
The fustest and mostest
To hit where they ain't.

L is Lajoie
Whom Clevelanders love,
Napoleon himself,
With glue in his glove.

M is for Matty,
Who carried a charm
In the form of an extra
Brain in his arm.

N is for Newsom,
Bobo's favorite kin.
If you ask how he's here,
He talked himself in.

O is for Ott
Of the restless right foot.
When he leaned on the pellet,
The pellet stayed put.

P is for Plank,
The arm of the A's;
When he tangled with Matty
Games lasted for days.

Q is Don Quixote
Cornelius Mack;
Neither Yankees nor years
Can halt his attack.

R is for Ruth.
To tell you the truth,
There's no more to be said,
Just R is for Ruth.

S is for Speaker,
Swift center-field tender;
When the ball saw him coming,
It yelled, "I surrender."

T is for Terry
The Giant from Memphis
Whose 400 average
You can't overemphis.

U would be Ubbell
If Carl were a cockney;
We say Hubbell and baseball
Like football and Rockne.

V is for Vance
The Dodgers' own Dazzy;
None of his rivals
Could throw as fast as he.

W, Wagner,
The bowlegged beauty;
Short was closed to all traffic
With Honus on duty.

X is the first
Of two x's in Foxx
Who was right behind Ruth
With his powerful soxx.

Y is for Young
The magnificent Cy;
People batted against him,
But I never knew why.

Z is for Zenith,
The summit of fame.
These men are up there,
These men are the game.

47

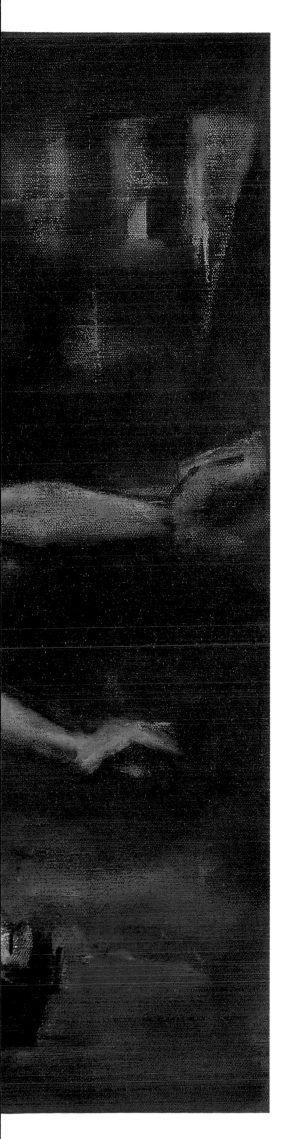

Hit & Run
by John Dobbs, 1982–96.

The Base Stealer

◆

ROBERT FRANCIS

Poised between going on and back, pulled
Both ways taut like a tightrope-walker,
Fingertips pointing the opposites,
Now bouncing tiptoe like a dropped ball
Or a kid skipping rope, come on, come on,
Running a scattering of steps sidewise,
How he teeters, skitters, tingles, teases,
Taunts them, hovers like an ecstatic bird,
He's only flirting, crowd him, crowd him,
Delicate, delicate, delicate, delicate—now!

Ballgloves

◆

RON McFARLAND

The baseball glove you lost that afternoon
in a sun-crazed field gone mad with dandelions
was mine. In my sophomore yearbook you can
find it tucked under my arm just below
my smile of phony confidence.
Does it look like I've made the team?
My best friend, who dreamed of himself
dreaming of baseball, has just been killed
driving his father's big blue Oldsmobile.

We went back to the field and searched
as the sun burned out and my rage
and your tears cooled, and the dandelions
quietly closed in on themselves.
At a garage sale a few weeks later
I found a ballglove with that same
sweat-leather smell and bought it for a song,
not that my old glove could be replaced,
but as a way of erasure. I sat that whole
long season on the bench, my ballglove
growing stiff, the pocket gone hollow.

The next day I bought you a brand-new glove
which you have long since lost yourself,
I guess, without a second thought.
My first baseball glove, an old Spalding
my uncle used when he played Class D one season
for the Washington Senators, swallowed my hand,
and no amount of neatsfoot oil could soften its
hard luck. Where did I lose that sweet old
patch of leather? In what bright golden
world of sun-struck dandelions?

Jump High at Second by Vincent Scilla, 1991.

[FOLLOWING PAGES]
Recalling the Game
by Bill Williams, 1993.

51

Louisville Slugger

◆

BOB GREENE

AT THE NEWSPAPER where I work we have a rule that staff members are not allowed to accept any gift of significant value from an outside source. The rule probably makes sense; its purpose is to prevent potential news sources from trying to influence news coverage through the bestowing of lavish presents.

But I recently received something in the mail from an outside company, and if the newspaper makes me give it back they're going to have to drag me out of here kicking and screaming and holding on to it for dear life.

The package was long and narrow. I opened it. Inside was something that brought tears to my eyes and a funny feeling to my throat:

A Louisville Slugger baseball bat—a Bob Greene autographed model.

For five minutes I sat there looking at it and caressing it and speaking softly to it.

There, in the middle of the barrel, was the Louisville Slugger logo, and the famous copyrighted slogan: "Powerized." There, next to the logo, was the trademark of the Hillerich & Bradsby Co., which manufactures Louisville Sluggers.

And there—right at the end of the barrel—were the words PERSONAL MODEL—LOUISVILLE SLUGGER. And where Mickey Mantle's or Hank Aaron's autograph ought to be, the script words "Bob Greene."

I suppose there must be some item that an American boy might treasure more fiercely than a Louisville Slugger with his own signature on it, but I can't think of one. For all of us who grew up on sandlots and playgrounds, gripping Louisville Sluggers bearing the autographs of major league stars, the thought of owning one with our own name on the barrel is almost too much to comprehend.

In the box with the Louisville Slugger was a letter from John A. Hillerich III, president of Hillerich & Bradsby. In the letter Hillerich said that this is the centennial year for Louisville Sluggers; the first one was manufactured in the spring of 1884. Thus, the enclosed bat—a memento of the 100th anniversary.

When I started to show my new bat to people, the response I got was interesting. Women seemed not to care too much; generally they said something like, "Oh, a baseball bat." They would inspect it a little more closely, and then say, "What's your name doing on it?"

But men—men were a different story. First they would see the bat.

They'd say something like, "A real Louisville Slugger. That's great." Invariably they would lift it up and go into a batting stance—perhaps for the first time in twenty or thirty years. Then they would roll the bat around in their hands—and finally they would see the signature.

That's when they'd get faint in the head. They would look as if they were about to swoon. Their eyes would start to resemble pinwheels. And in reverential whispers, they would say: "That is the most wonderful thing I have ever seen. Your own name on a Louisville Slugger. You are so lucky."

For it is true: a Louisville Slugger, for the American male, is a talisman— a piece of property that carries such symbolic weight and meaning that words of description do not do it justice. I have a friend who has two photographs mounted above his desk at work. One photo shows Elvis Presley kissing a woman. The other shows Ted Williams kissing his Louisville Slugger. No one ever asks my friend the meaning of those pictures; the meaning, of course, is quite clear without any explanation.

Hillerich & Bradsby has a photo in its archives that is similarly moving. In the photo, Babe Ruth and Lou Gehrig are standing in a batting cage. Gehrig, a wide smile on his face, is examining the bat. Perhaps you could find another photo that contains three figures more holy to the American male than those three—Ruth, Gehrig, and a Louisville Slugger—but I don't know where you'd look.

Hillerich & Bradsby has some intriguing figures and facts about Louisville Sluggers. The company manufactures approximately one million of them each year. That requires the use of about two hundred thousand trees each baseball season; the company owns five thousand acres of timberland in Pennsylvania and New York to provide the trees. Ash timber is the wood of choice for Louisville Sluggers. Years ago, the wood of choice was hickory.

According to the company, a professional baseball player uses an average of seventy-two bats each season—which comes as a surprise to those of us who always envisioned a major leaguer using the same special good-luck bat for years on end. The company says that, during World War II, some American sporting goods found their way to a German prison camp in Upper Silesia; the American prisoners of war there reportedly cried at the sight of the Louisville Sluggers. During the Korean War, an American soldier reportedly dashed out of his trench during a firefight to retrieve a Louisville Slugger he had left out in the open before the battle began.

◆   ◆   ◆

AS I SIT HERE TYPING THIS, a colleague—a male—has just walked up next to my computer terminal, lifted my Louisville Slugger to his shoulder, and gone into a batter's crouch. In a moment, if I'm right, he'll start examining the bat—and in another moment he'll see the autograph.

I can't wait. ❖

Harry H. Davis Louisville Slugger bat decal.

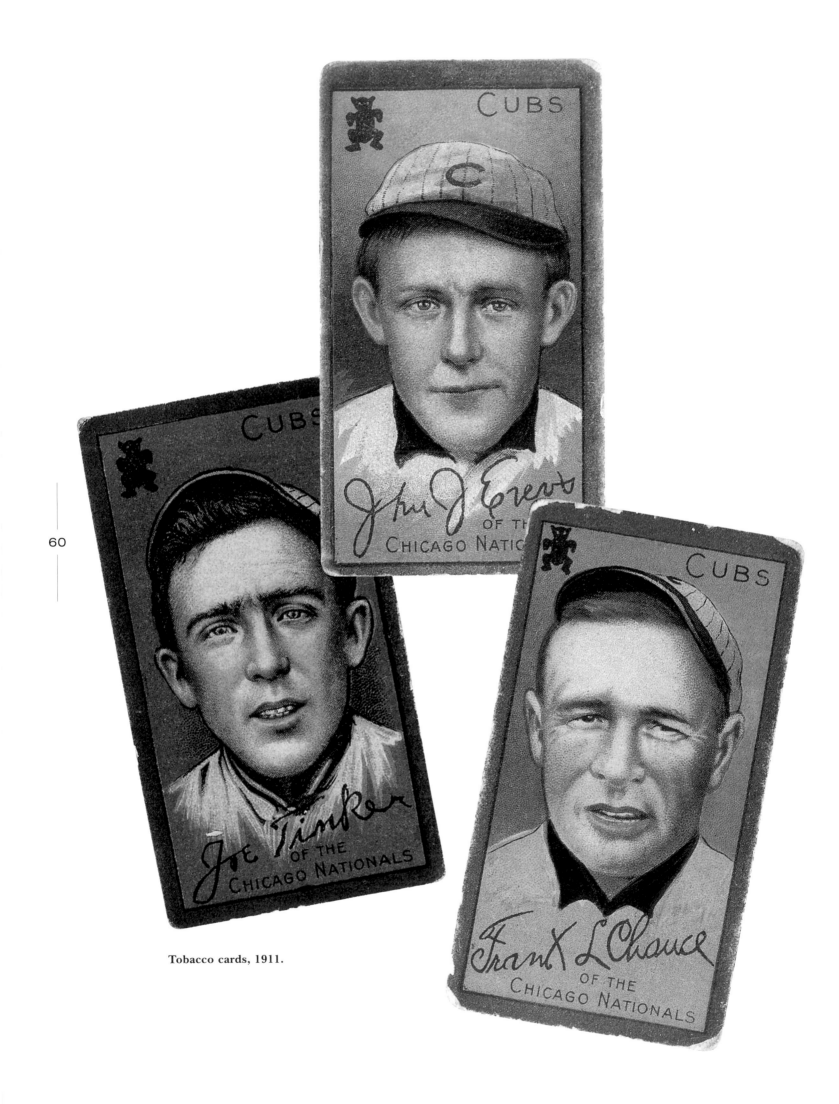

Tobacco cards, 1911.

Baseball's Sad Lexicon

◆

FRANKLIN PIERCE ADAMS

These are the saddest of possible words,
"Tinker to Evers to Chance."
Trio of Bear Cubs and fleeter than birds,
"Tinker to Evers to Chance."
Ruthlessly pricking our gonfalon bubble,
Making a Giant hit into a double,
Words that are weighty with nothing but trouble,
"Tinker to Evers to Chance."

MAY 1936
25 CENTS

The American LEGION MONTHLY

The American Legion magazine cover, May 1936.

[FOLLOWING PAGES]
**Prang Lithography Company
advertising poster, 1887.**

From
A Bush League Hero

◆

EDNA FERBER

ANY MAN WHO CAN LOOK HANDSOME in a dirty baseball suit is an Adonis. There is something about the baggy pants, and the Micawber-shaped collar, and the skull-fitting cap, and the foot or so of tan, or blue, or pink undershirt sleeve sticking out at the arms, that just naturally kills a man's best points. Then too, a baseball suit requires so much in the matter of leg. Therefore, when I say that Rudie Schlachweiler was a dream even in his baseball uniform, with a dirty brown streak right up the side of his pants where he had slid for base, you may know that the girls camped on the grounds during the season.

During the summer months our ball park is to us what the Grand Prix is to Paris, or Ascot is to London. What care we that Evers gets seven thousand a year (or is it a month?); or that Chicago's new Southside ball park seats thirty-five thousand (or is it million?). Of what interest are such meager items compared with the knowledge that "Pug" Coulan, who plays short, goes with Undine Meyers, the girl up there in the eighth row, with the pink dress and the red roses on her hat? When "Pug" snatches a high one out of the firmament we yell with delight, and even as we yell we turn sideways to look up

and see how Undine is taking it. Undine's shining eyes are fixed on "Pug," and he knows it, stoops to brush the dust off his dirt-begrimed baseball pants, takes an attitude of careless grace and misses the next play.

Our grand-stand seats almost two thousand, counting the boxes. But only the snobs, and the girls with new hats, sit in the boxes. Box seats are comfortable, it is true, and they cost only an additional ten cents, but we have come to consider them undemocratic, and unworthy of true fans. Mrs. Freddy Van Dyne, who spends her winters in Egypt and her summers at the ball park, comes out to the game every afternoon in her automobile, but she never occupies a box seat; so why should we? She perches up in the grand-stand with the rest of the enthusiasts, and when Kelly puts one over she stands up and clinches her fists, and waves her arms and shouts with the best of 'em. She has even been known to cry, "Good eye! Good eye!" when things were at fever heat. The only really blasé individual in the ball park is Willie Grimes, who peddles ice-cream cones. For that matter, I once saw Willie turn a languid head to pipe, in his thin voice, "Give 'em a dark one, Dutch! Give 'em a dark one!" ❖

Standing Mitt with Ball by Claes Oldenburg, 1973.

Baseball Innovations

◆

ALBERT GOODWILL SPALDING

THE FIRST GLOVE I EVER SAW on the hand of a ball player in a game was worn by Charles C. Waite, in Boston, in 1875. He had come from New Haven and was playing at first base. The glove worn by him was of flesh color, with a large, round opening in the back. Now, I had for a good while felt the need of some sort of hand protection for myself. In those days clubs did not carry an extra carload of pitchers, as now. For several years I had pitched in every game played by the Boston team, and had developed severe bruises on the inside of my left hand. When it is recalled that every ball pitched had to be returned, and that every swift one coming my way, from infielders, outfielders or hot from the bat, must be caught or stopped, some idea may be gained of the punishment received.

Therefore, I asked Waite about his glove. He confessed that he was a bit ashamed to wear it, but had it on to save his hand. He also admitted that he had chosen a color as inconspicuous as possible, because he didn't care to attract attention. He added that the opening on the back was for purpose of ventilation.

Meanwhile my own hand continued to take its medicine with utmost regularity, occasionally being bored with a warm twister that hurt excruciatingly. Still, it was not until 1877 that I overcame my scruples against joining the "kid-glove aristocracy" by donning a glove. When I did at last decide to do so, I did not select a flesh-colored glove, but got a black one, and cut out as much of the back as possible to let the air in.

Happily, in my case, the presence of a glove did not call out the ridicule that had greeted Waite. I had been playing so long and had become so well known that the innovation seemed rather to evoke sympathy than hilarity. I found that the glove, thin as it was, helped considerably, and inserted one pad after another until a good deal of relief was afforded. If anyone wore a padded glove before this date I do not know it. The "pillow mitt" was a later innovation.

About this time, 1875–76, James Tyng, catcher for the Harvard Base Ball Club, appeared on the Boston grounds one day, and, stepping to his position, donned the first wire mask I had ever seen. This mask had been invented and patented by Mr. Fred W. Thayer, a Harvard player. . . . Like other protective innovations at that stage of the game, it was not at first well received by professionals. Our catcher, James White, was urged to try it, and after some coaxing consented. I pitched him a few balls, some of which he missed, and finally, becoming disgusted at being unable to see the ball readily, he tore off the mask and, hurling it toward the bench, went on without it.

This wire mask, with certain modifications, is the same that has been used by catchers ever since. ❖

THERE IS A PROVERB THAT GOES, "The best way out of a difficulty is through it." However, when that difficulty is a murderer's row line-up of batters, getting through it takes a long, long time. And with all due respect to other sports, the obligation to go through it is one of the maddening things that makes this game special. In baseball, you can't run out the clock.

Some face difficulty by putting up a fight. For instance, in a selection that follows, poet Tim Peeler pays homage to Curt Flood, who sacrificed his career to fight the reserve clause, which reduced players to property in the days before free agency. In another, Weldon Walker, one of the first black players in the major

Chapter III
SACRIFICES

leagues—sixty years before Jackie Robinson—protests the ban against his play.

For others it means a different kind of sacrifice. In William Brashler's *The Bingo Long Travelling All-Stars and Motor Kings* one sees a story common to all cultures and eras: talented individuals compelled to hide their superiority behind clown faces, at great personal cost.

In each case it's a trade-off, a compromise, the sort of mature choice that distinguishes adulthood from childhood. The title character of Percival Everett's novel *Suder*, cut loose from the safety of what he knows, begins a picaresque adventure. The characters of Mark Harris's *Bang the Drum Slowly* retreat into the safety of the game's rules and schedules to deny the inevitability of death.

For everyone—even baseball players—carefree days give way to complicated and darker times. At times like that, whatever you think about the best way out of difficulty, you must admire the blind determination displayed by the teammates described by Philip Gerard in "Hardball." All these stories point to the facts of the game: At some point you are going to be in trouble; and when that moment comes, you better believe you can throw that last strike or make that clutch hit.

[OPPOSITE]
3000
by Jon Lezinsky, May 1993.

Difficult moments

70

"I'm not concerned with your liking or disliking me. All I ask is that you respect me as a human being."

—JACKIE ROBINSON

I Have Grievances

◆

WELDON WALKER

[*Walker, one of the first African-Americans in professional baseball, played for Akron of the Tri-State League in 1887. After protests by white players, he and the other African-American players were barred from the league, prompting this 1888 letter.*]

To George McDermitt, President of the Tri-State League

I HAVE GRIEVANCES, SIR. I question whether my individual loss serves the public good. I write you not because I have been denied making my bread and butter, but in the hope that the league's action will be reversed. The rule that you have passed is a public disgrace! It casts derision on the laws of Ohio, the voice of the people, which says that all men are equal. There is now the same accommodation for colored and white men and women in your ball parks, and the same disposition is made of the moneys of both. I would suggest to your honorable body that if your rule is not repealed, you should make it criminal for black men and women to be admitted to your ball park.

There should be some sounder cause for dismissal, such as lack of intelligence or misbehavior. Ability, intelligence, should be recognized first, last and at all times by everyone. I ask this question—why was this rule passed?

[*McDermitt never answered Walker's letter.*]

[OPPOSITE]
Turning Pale
by Jon Lezinsky, 1996.

The Bingo Long Travelling All-Stars and Motor Kings

◆

WILLIAM BRASHLER

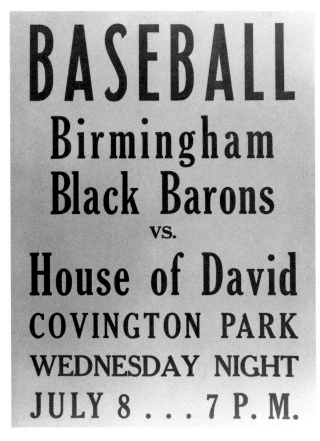

Negro League game poster.

"YOU BOYS DOING GOOD, real good," Lionel said to Bingo as they walked from the field after the game. "You got class and you got talent like nobody I seen around. You play it right, Bingo, and you ain't going to be able to keep the people from giving you their money."

Lionel had contacted some of the big promoters in the Midwest and set up a half dozen games in Cleveland, Toledo, and Chicago. These were all league towns, so the All-Stars had to work around schedules to get their games. After Chicago they could hit Milwaukee and then head west across Wisconsin and Iowa.

"You got to watch out for the other barnstormers like Max Helverton's Hooley Speedballers and them white teams from Michigan, them House of David boys with the beards," Lionel told Bingo. "You can't follow them because you lose the edge on the towns. You can play them but when you is done you should go in the opposite direction. It ain't trouble; it's just good business. And remember too, Bingo, that you got to hit those towns when they ain't doing nothing big like harvesting or something because then you lose your crowd. Otherwise they going to welcome you like you was a circus."

Bingo already knew most of what Lionel was telling him, but he listened anyway because Lionel had run almost every kind of travelling show around. Lionel helped him get up some paper for advertising and letters to send to town post offices announcing the All-Stars' arrival. The night before the team took off for Cleveland, Bingo sat down with Lionel and went over possible routines and antics to please the crowds. "Remember," Lionel said, "ain't nothing around pleases more than good ball playing. Better than folks has ever seen. They remember it because it *amazes* them. Yeah, it does."

Bingo called a meeting that night after the players had come in from the Chop House.

"I been doing some talking and some planning and I'm ready to present you with what we going to be doing on this tour. Now you all know how to play and how to look good like we did yesterday with the Giants. And when we be playing the big teams like the Detroit Cubans and the Velvets in Chicago and around in there we won't have no trouble either because they is our own people watching and we know what they likes. But some of you ain't been past Chicago and you don't know what happens out there. In them dog towns we got to play it with our nose. We got to please the people who works them farms. And if they want to see us clown then we clown them until they dead. But if they want to see us play straight then we do and take our chances against what they got. We just can't be looking bad or nonchalant or no good. Because then they be calling us a bunch of shuffles and they ain't going to be throwing their quarters in our socks. So they ain't much we can do until we see what the situation is but we got to be ready. We got to be polite and cheerful all the time even when we ain't feeling it. If we get trouble we just be leaving by the back way and getting on down the road with our hands in our pockets and whistling like we stole the lady's pie. Now that is something I thought I should say right off so you know where this team stands. Lionel say if we play it right we going to

take their money. I think he's right because he been around. He takes some lumps too, yes he does. But that's what I got to say."

He stopped and wiped his mouth. Nobody said anything. Then he went on.

"We going to be playing a lot of white outfits too. Some of you ain't played much against white so you got to be prepared. They take what they can out of you if you don't be on your guard. They going to slide into your leg and step on your foot if you leave it out there in plain sight. They going to be saying the same old things to rattle you and get you to forget how to play right. But they ain't nothing. They got to pitch to you when you up to the plate. I hit everything a white pitch can throw and they don't like it but they can't do much but run after it. So that's how we play them. You keep your heads turned behind your back all the time for something sneaking up on you. That's the way you play white."

Bingo stopped again and waited for a reaction. He could feel himself getting excited. The players sat and looked at him, blinking their eyes. Louis Keystone yawned.

"That was a nice speech, Bingo. Real nice," Leon finally said. ❖

Curt Flood

◆

TIM PEELER

try to tell 'em Curt,
how you crowned their wallets,
climbed courtroom steps
for them,
swallowed that black ball,
a scapegoat out to pasture.
they don't remember,
can't remember
the trash you ate,
your greedy headlines,
the slope of your career.

you are a ghost at barterer's wing,
your smokey gray eyes
are two extra zeroes
on every contract.

Baseball Noir by **Robert Valdes, 1996.**

Dugout at Night: Late Innings
by John Hull, 1990.

From
Bang the Drum Slowly

◆

MARK HARRIS

WE STARTED FAST in the second game. It was raining a little. Sid hit a home run in the first with Pasquale aboard, Number 42, the first home run he hit since August 17, according to the paper, and Bruce shook his hand at the plate, and Sid stopped and told Bruce, "Wipe off your bat," and Bruce looked at his bat and at Sid, not understanding, not feeling the rain, and Sid took the bat and wiped it off, and Bruce whistled a single in left, the last base hit he ever hit, and made his turn and went back and stood with one foot on the bag and said something to Clint, and Clint yelled for Dutch, and Dutch went out, and they talked. I do not know what about. Dutch only said to me, "Pick up your sign off the bench," and he sent for Doc, and Doc sat in the alley behind the dugout and waited, and the boys sometimes strolled back and sat beside him, asking him questions, "What does he have?" and such as that. They smoked back there, which Dutch does not like you to, saying, "Smoking ain't learning. Sitting on the bench and watching is learning," but he said nothing that day. You knew he wouldn't.

Washington begun stalling like mad in the third, hoping for heavy rain before it become official, claiming it was raining, though the umps ruled it was not. Sy Sibley was umping behind the plate. They stepped out between pitches and wiped off their bat and tied their shoe and blew their nose and gouged around in their eye, saying, "Something is in my eye," and Sy said, "Sure, your eyeball," and they stepped back in. As soon as they stepped back in again I pitched.

He never knew what was coming, curve ball or what. "Just keep your meat hand out of the way," I said, and he said he would but did not. It did not register. He was catching by habit and memory, only knowing that when the pitcher threw it you were supposed to stop it and throw it back, and if a fellow hit a foul ball you were supposed to whip off your mask and collar it, and if a man was on base you were supposed to keep him from going on to the next one. You play ball all your life until a day comes when you do not know what you are doing, but you do it anyhow, working through a fog, not remembering anything but only knowing who people were by how they moved, this fellow the hitter, this the pitcher, and if you hit the ball you run to the right, and then when you got there you asked Clint Strap were you safe or out because you do not know yourself. There was a fog settling down over him.

I do not know how he got through it. I do not even know how yours truly got through it. I do not remember much. It was 3-0 after 4 ½, official now, and now we begun stalling, claiming it was raining, claiming the ball was wet and we were libel to be beaned, which Washington said would make no difference to fellows with heads as hard as us. Eric Bushell said it to me in the fifth when I complained the ball was wet, and I stepped out and started laughing, "Ha ha ha ho ho ho, ha ha ha," doubling over and laughing, and Sy Sibley said, "Quit stalling," and I said I could not help it if Bushell was going to say such humorous things to me and make me laugh. "Tell him to stop," I said. "Ha ha ha ho ho ho ha ha ha."

"What did he say?" said Sy, and I told him, telling him very slow, telling him who Eric Bushell was and who I was, the crowd thinking it was an argument and booing Sy. "Forget it," said he. "Get back in and hit."

"You mean bat," said Bushell. "He never hits," and I begun laughing again, stepping out and saying how could a man bat with this fellow behind me that if the TV people knew how funny he was they would make him an offer.

"Hit!" said Sy. "Bat! Do not stall."

"Who is stalling?" said I, and I stepped back in, the rain coming a little heavier now.

I threw one pitch in the top of the seventh, a ball, wide, to Billy Linenthal. I guess I remember. Bruce took it backhand and stood up and slowly raised his hand and took the ball out of his mitt and started to toss it back, aiming very carefully at my chin, like Red told him to, and then everybody begun running, for the rain come in for sure now, and he seen everybody running, but he did not run, only stood there. I

started off towards the dugout, maybe as far as the baseline, thinking he was following, and then I seen that he was not. I seen him standing looking for somebody to throw to, the last pitch he ever caught, and I went back for him, and Mike and Red were there when I got there, and Mike said, "It is over, son," and he said "Sure" and trotted on in.

◆　◆　◆

In the hospital me and Mike and Red waited in the waiting room for word, telling them 1,000 times, "Keep us posted," which they never done and you had to run down the hall and ask, and then when you asked they never *knew* anything, and for all you could tell they were never *doing* anything neither, only looking at his chart, standing outside his door and looking at his chart and maybe whistling or kidding the nurses until I really got quite annoyed.

He was unconscious. Around midnight he woke up, and they said one of us could see him, the calmest, and I went, and he only said "Howdy," but very weak, not saying it, really, only his lips moving. He looked at me a long time and worked up his strength and said again, "Howdy, Arthur," and the doctor said, "He does not know you," and I said he did, for he always called me "Arthur." Then he lifted off again.

They told me take his clothes away, and I took them, his uniform and cap and socks and shoes, and I rolled them up with his belt around them and carried them back out. Red and Mike went pale when they seen me. They went pale every little while all night, every time a phone rung or a doctor passed through. "Relax," said I. "He is not dying."

"You never seen anybody die," said Red.

"I seen them in the movies," I said.

"It ain't the same," he said.

"He will not die," said Mike. "He will only pass on."

We went out and got something to eat. It was still raining, and we walked a long ways before we found a place open. It was very quiet in the streets. We ate in one of these smoky little places, everything fried. The paper said MAMMOTHS COP 2, GOLDMAN SWATS, 42ND, and there was a picture of Sid crossing the plate and Bruce shaking his hand. "Then he hit," I said.

"And then he did not know what happened without going back and asking Clint," said Red.

"It is sad," said Mike. "It makes you wish to cry."

"It is sad," said Red. "It makes you wish to laugh."

We went back in the waiting room and stretched on the couches and slept. While we were asleep somebody threw a blanket over me, and over Red and Mike as well. I don't know who. When we woke up the sun was shining, and I went down the hall and asked, and they looked at his chart and said he was fine, and I heard him singing then, singing, "As I was a-walking the streets of Laredo, as I walked out in Laredo one day, I spied a young cowboy all wrapped in white linen, all wrapped in white linen and cold as the clay," and I run back for Red and Mike, and they heard me come running and went all pale again, and I said, "Come with me," and we went back down the hall again. You could hear him even further down now, for he sung louder, "It was once in the saddle I used to go dashing, once in the saddle I used to go gay, first down to Rosie's and then to the card house, shot in the breast and am dying today." We stood and listened and then run in, and he stopped singing and tried sitting up, but he was too weak, and we said, "Get on up out of there now and back to work," and "This sure is a lazy man's way of drawing pay for no work," and he said, "Did anybody bring my chews?"

"I will go get them," said Mike, and he went back to the hotel and brung them, and clothes as well, saying, "I hope I brung the right combination," and Bruce said "Yes." He never cares about the combination anyhow, only grabs the nearest. If I did not shuffle his suits around he would wear the same one every day.

We hung in the hospital. Dutch called from St. Louis around supper, glad to hear that all was well again, and he told Red why not come out now, as long as the worst was over. "Business before pleasure," said Red, and he went.

He was so weak he even got tired chewing, shoving it over in his cheek and leaving it there, and his hands shook. He could not hold the newspaper nor his knife and fork but would eat a little and lay back again, saying, "No doubt I will pep up and be back in action again in no time," and we said he would, me and Mike and the doctors and nurses as well, though we knew he would not. Maybe I never seen a man die and wouldn't know if I did, but I knew when a man was not libel to be back in action very soon. ❖

81

[FOLLOWING PAGES]
Batting Cage
by John Hull, 1989.

Sign for My Father,
Who Stressed the Bunt

◆

DAVID BOTTOMS

84

On the rough diamond,
the hand-cut field below the dog lot and barn,
we rehearsed the strict technique
of bunting. I watched from the infield,
the mound, the backstop
as your left hand climbed the bat, your legs
and shoulders squared toward the pitcher.
You could drop it like a seed
down either base line. I admired your style,
but not enough to take my eyes off the bank
that served as our center-field fence.

Years passed, three leagues of organized ball,
no few lives. I could homer
into the garden beyond the bank,
into the left-field lot of Carmichael Motors,
and still you stressed the same technique,
the crouch and spring, the lead arm absorbing
just enough impact. That whole tiresome pitch
about basics never changing,
and I never learned what you were laying down.

Like a hand brushed across the bill of a cap,
let this be the sign
I'm getting a grip on the sacrifice.

i.vi/pitcher 5   C. Hobson

The Hummer

◆

WILLIAM MATTHEWS

First he drew a strike zone
on the toolshed door, and then
he battered against it all summer
a balding tennis ball, wetted
in a puddle he tended under
an outdoor faucet: that way
he could see, at first, exactly
where each pitch struck.
Late in the game the door
was solidly blotched and
calling the corners was fierce
enough moral work for any
man he might grow up to be.
His stark rules made it hard
to win, and made him finish
any game he started, no matter
if he'd lost it early.
Some days he pitched
six games, the last in dusk,
in tears, in rage, in the blue
blackening joy of obsession.
If he could have been also
the batter, he would have been,
trying to stay alive. Twenty-
seven deaths a game and all
of them his. For a real game
the time it takes is listed
in the box score, the obituary.
What he loved was mowing
them down. Thwap. Thwap.
Then one thwap low and outside.
And finally the hummer.
It made him grunt to throw it,
as if he'd tried to hold it
back, but it escaped. Thwap.

[OPPOSITE]
Leonardo Series: OUT/pitcher 5
by Charles Hobson, 1990.

From
Suder

◆

PERCIVAL EVERETT

SO, I'M UP AT THE PLATE in the top of the ninth and the first pitch is, I grant you, an honest-to-God textbook strike and the fat umpire's backwards dance and that turn to the right he manages don't offend me at all. And then the second pitch comes whistling in way inside and I hear that fat man in blue yell, "*Steee-rike!*" and I turn to catch the tail end of his routine and I just can't believe it. So, I flip the bat in my hand like a baton, as is my custom, and step up to him, face to face, and give him the questioning eye.

There he is right in front of me, behind that foam-filled apron, and he yells, "Strike!"

"That was way inside," I tell him, "I could feel it on my pants."

"Strike," he repeats and lets out this little shit-eating grin and I really want to hit him and I tell myself not to and turn away.

"Blind bastard," I says under my breath.

And he says to me, "If you can't—"

I cut him off: "Why don't you go read up on the strike zone."

He looks at me and yells, "Play ball!" Then when I'm stepping into the box he says, "That's two, Suder."

And I ignore him. The next pitch is so inside that the catcher leaves his perch to get it and I know because I follow the ball all the way, don't even move my bat, but as sure as anything that fat umpire does his Fred Astaire and calls another strike. So, I'm out and when I'm walking away I mutter, "Why don't you just put on one of their uniforms!" And I'm still holding the bat clenched in my fists when David Nicks flies to center for the third out.

The pitcher finishes his warm-ups and the ball gets passed all around and fast Eddie Ramos is walking up to the plate swinging a bat with a lead doughnut on it. Lou Tyler, our manager, is yelling that we're up one run and that we should hold them. "Three up, three down," he says. "Three up, three down." Then he yells to me, "Suder! Suder!" and I turn to see him make like he's bunting with an invisible bat. "Watch the bunt!" he yells. "Watch the bunt!" It strikes me that he sometimes says things twice and I imagine it's a fancy way of stuttering and, heeding his words, I step on down the third-base line toward the batter.

Strike by Jacob Lawrence, 1949.

The first pitch is outside, but I see his left hand sneak up along the wood and I know he wants to bunt and I get ready. On the next pitch he does bunt and I run for it and the catcher runs for it and the pitcher runs for it and we all stop dead cold like it's something nasty we want somebody else to pick up. Finally, I pick it up, pump once—the asshole pitcher is in the way—and throw it to first, but I'm too late. So, the tying run is on first and I look up at the board and see I'm being charged with an error. The next guy up doesn't bunt, he just tags that first pitch and sends it airmail special delivery over the left-field fence, the old Green Monster, and the game is over and we lose and ain't nothing left but the crying and accusing. I close my eyes for a second and then I take to the showers.

So, I come out of the shower and slide into my Jockey shorts and sit down in front of my locker with my face in my hands. I think to myself that all I want to do is get stinking drunk, when I see Lou Tyler turning the corner and heading down the aisle toward me. He comes and sits beside me, straddles the wooden chair, and pushes the brim of his cap up.

"We all have slumps," he says and I'm pulling on my socks, half listening to him, and he goes on, "but you got to break out of this one soon."

I look over at him and I ask, "Did you see what they was calling strikes out there?"

"So you had a bad call."

"A bad call? I suppose I really made that error out there, too." I look away from him and shake my head.

"Okay, a couple of bad calls."

"Jesus," I says.

"Truth of the matter is, Craig, that you have to straighten up and fly right." And he slaps me on the back and tells me to get dressed.

I watch him walk away and then I slam the locker. "Yeah, straighten up and fly right," I says to myself, "fly right."

◆　　◆　　◆

WE GET TO THE AIRPORT and we're boarding the plane when Tuck McShane, the trainer, comes up to me. "How's the leg?" he wants to know.

"Ain't nothing wrong with my leg," I says, sitting down.

He sits beside me. "I thought I saw you favoring your left leg last night."

"Nope."

"I'm glad you're sitting by the window." He looks past me out over the wing. It's common knowledge that old Tuck gets dizzy when he stands tippy-toed.

"What you studying on so hard?" he asks me and then, before I can answer, "Don't worry, you'll pick up. You'll play a lot better once you relax. You oughta try some breathing exercises." He inhales deeply and lets it out.

I look back out the window and watch the flaps as we take off and I see a bird and I begin to wish I could fly up high and all without the aid of a machine.

As we're climbing out of the plane in Baltimore, old Tuck turns to me. "It's your right leg, ain't it? Want me to take a look?"

"Ain't nothing wrong with my leg," I says.

We check into the hotel and David Nicks and I go to our room. While David is in the bathroom I call my wife and she's sounding a little down, so I ask her what's wrong.

"Peter came home the other day and he'd been fighting," she tells me.

"He's a seven-year-old boy, honey," I says, "they fight sometimes."

"You don't understand. This is the third time this week."

"Maybe somebody's picking on him. He's gotta stand up for himself."

"He says the boys at day camp tease him about you, the way you've been playing."

I hear this and I don't know what to say.

"Craig?"

"What's he doing in that school yard, anyway? It's summer, he should be out playing in the grass. Listen, I've got to go. David wants the phone."

"Okay, I love you."

"Me, too."

I go out and get drunk enough to embarrass a few dead relatives. I'm still drinking and I'm feeling pretty bad seeing as we just dropped three straight to Boston and this fella recognizes me. "Ain't you Craig Suder?"

I nod. I don't even look at him, just keep my eyes on the bar and nod.

He starts to laugh and talk about how we got our butts whipped and I just keep looking at the bar, nodding. Then he says, "If you was outta the lineup, Seattle might win a few."

He still ain't got to me and I'm still nodding.

He sorta calls one of his buddies over and they're standing on either side of me and the first fella says, "Black boys ain't got no business in baseball no way."

Well, at this I turn and look at him and the next thing I know I'm coming to in an alley with my face in some garbage. I get up and make my way to the hotel. ❖

Hardball

◆

PHILIP GERARD

AFTER COLLEGE, when I lived in Burlington, Vermont, and tended bar at The Last Chance Saloon, only a few rough blocks above the tank farms and barge docks on Lake Champlain, I got recruited to join a baseball team in one of the small outlying towns. We played other town teams, usually on weekends. Our home field was built on the edge of a granite quarry—beyond the outfield fence was oblivion. The first practice, as I trotted out to my position in left field, the centerfielder warned me: "Don't go diving over that fence after a ball—it's a long way down."

I leaned over the chain-link fence and stared down a hundred vertical feet onto solid rock, flat and smooth where the gray stone had been carved away in great square slabs.

The infield was rock-hard basepaths and scalped grass across which grounders zipped like bullets. The pitcher's mound was high and the batter's box was a ditch. Whoever had designed this baseball diamond had created an obstacle at every position.

It fit the country, a place of hard-scrabble farms and bone-cracking winters, deep in recession. Half the men on the team were out of work; the others scrambled between two or three different jobs, trying to make ends meet. They stacked groceries or repaired cars all day and then spent their evenings splitting firewood for sale. In the winter they drove snowplows and repaired chain saws. But those were just jobs—not who they were. They were ballplayers, serious about the game.

Our player-manager and catcher was a muscle-bound plumber who shaved his head and sharpened his cleats with a file before each game. He had a habit of firing the ball back sidearm to the pitcher after each pitch, daring him to catch it. That first day, as we loosened up, throwing and catching, he burned one into my glove so hard my palm stung. He grinned at me through missing front teeth. "We play hardball, son," he said. "Got it?"

"Right." I loped out to shag flies, wary of the low fence and the long drop.

The outfield captain had come up through the Yankee farm system with Mickey Rivers. Rivers went north to star in the Majors, but our captain

Mine Baseball by Mervin Jules, 1937.

ended up roaming semi-pro outfields with an attitude. He played mad. He swung at pitches like a man murdering his wife's lover with an axe. When he chased the ball into left field, I cleared out of his way. I always had the uneasy feeling that one day he was going to take a running leap over that fence after a fly ball and catch it on the way down. That he wanted to do it.

Our pitching ace and his 85-mile-an-hour fast ball had been drafted by the Pirates straight out of high school—then they released him after a single season, my teammates said, because he was psychologically unstable and a menace. He'd get that light in his eye, and he wouldn't take signals from the catcher. He wouldn't take signals from anybody.

He always pitched with a manic grin on his face. His control was erratic—or so he pretended. I think now he always knew exactly what he was doing, and the crazy act was just a way to psyche out the hitters. He'd wing pitches over the backstop just to keep the batters guessing. The more furious the batter became, the bigger he grinned. He seemed to like keeping everything—his fastball, the batter, the fielders, the game—just on the verge of going out of control. If the other team got a rally going, he would knock down the next hitter, and no umpire ever called him on it.

In our league, you had to actually injure another player to get thrown out of the game, and then it was even money.

The trademark of our second baseman, a spray hitter, was the headfirst slide—a dangerous play, since on a close throw your face winds up dueling with the baseman's knees, fists, and spikes. His face and arms were always cut and bruised, as if he spent his time brawling in taverns and not hitting to the opposite field.

The other players were equally eccentric—aging jocks who had once had a shot at the big time and blown it, holding on, doing it the hard way, playing for keeps.

In that league, we slid high and threw low. No game was complete without a knockdown collision at homeplate or a free-for-all at second base. More than once I came home with blood on my jersey.

I'd never been better than a mediocre player. I had no dreams of glory, but I've always enjoyed the game. I could pound out doubles, hit a long ball once in awhile, and catch anything in the outfield that landed in front of me. But I couldn't hit a really slick curveball, and I couldn't make the over-the-shoulder catch going away.

In that league, though, pitchers preferred to smoke the ball right down the middle of the plate—mano a mano—and I could hit a fastball all day long. Defensively, I played with my back to the fence, out of pure terror. I ran in on everything. So I had the season of my life. That summer, I was powerlifting, and I handled a 35-inch Louisville Slugger easily. I rapped out vicious grounders that sent shortstops sprawling. I ricocheted frozen ropes off the centerfield fence. That troubled crew made me believe I was better than I was, and I played harder than I ever had. We slugged our way to the playoffs, in which I doubled in the winning run.

Like every contest in which winning carries virtually no reward, we fought the championship game out hard and for keeps. At long last, the classic moment arrived—how could it not, that season? Two out, bottom of the ninth, down by a run, two men on base. I stepped up to the plate. The pitcher winged a fastball down the alley, and I nicked it up over the backstop. He came right back at me with another fastball on the corner, and I slammed it down the third-base line, just foul. The thin crowd in the bleachers was going nuts. I stepped out of the box to whack the mud off my cleats, took a breath, then stepped in.

I remember even now the quality of the light—that clear Vermont light, crisp as green apples, the field of vision opening beyond the scowling pitcher and the crouching infielders and the outfielders kicking at the grass like horses, beyond the silver top rail of the fence into absolute blue sky.

My wrists were loose and the bat felt weightless. Everybody was shouting—my teammates, the other players, the wives and girlfriends and younger brothers in the stands—and their voices blended into a surfy, incomprehensible murmur, and I had a clear vision of what was about to happen: The pitcher was rattled. His next fastball would sail in a little too high. I would get around on it quick and sock it into left centerfield.

Watch it arc over the fence.

Not start my homerun trot toward first base until the white ball disappeared into the quarry.

The pitcher wound up. His arm whipped past his ear in a blur. The ball came in high and fast, just as I had predicted. I dug in my back foot, took a short step with the front one, and swung from the heels. The power came out of my thighs and up my back and down from my shoulders into my thick arms and the wrists snapped around quick and the bat sang through a perfect arc.

But it was a curveball. It tailed magnificently toward my knees. I missed it by a mile.

I swung so hard, I cracked the thin handle of the barrel-heavy bat. When I swatted it against the ground in disgust, it busted clean in two.

◆　◆　◆

A FEW MONTHS LATER, I left Vermont. I played another season with a town team in Delaware—a young, careless bunch who played, not hardball, but baseball. I never again played under such low skies, never again played with such desperate men, never again hit so hard or wanted to win so badly that, the night before a game, my stomach hurt.

Whenever I watch a big league game on TV now, I can't help but think of all the guys who didn't make it. Who almost made it. Who couldn't hit the slick curveball. Whose defensive game was one step too slow, or whose character had some hairline fracture that revealed itself under the stress of pro competition as under an X-ray. Who had been the boys with the high expectations, the heroes of their high schools, the older brothers their parents always bragged about, the boys all the other boys wanted to be like, who ached for glory, but whose imagined future never came true. Who never learned properly how to be men—how to take from disappointment hope, and from failure the dignity of their secret character.

I imagine them out there, roaming ugly hardscrabble fields in far-flung country places, throwing low and sliding high, inflicting as much pain on each other and themselves as they possibly can, season after season, waiting to take that last great flying leap over the outfield fence into oblivion. ❖

The Red Wings at Silver Stadium
by Helen Fabi Smagorinsky, 1983.

Chapter IV

THE CYCLE

ASK PEOPLE ABOUT THE FIRST real baseball game they saw and you'll hear about the parent or grandparent or uncle or aunt who took them to the ballpark. Baseball connects generations. "The game of baseball has always been linked in my mind," wrote historian and Brooklyn Dodger fan Doris Kearns Goodwin, "with the mystic texture of childhood, with the sounds and smells of summer nights and with memories of my father."

Baseball brings people together when nothing else can, as Donald Hall notes in "Baseball and the Meaning of Life." The game's constancy makes this possible. The sudden drop of a curveball, as tough to hit now as it ever was, holds the same fascination for an adult of fifty as for a child of five. "I guess it is childish," says a character in the movie *City Slickers*, "but when I was about eighteen and my dad and I couldn't communicate about anything at all, we could still talk about baseball. Now that—that was real."

The game also measures the stages of our own lives. We might look forward to the infinite possibilities, or backward as we reckon the losses and unpredicted twists—as poet Ron Smith does when enjoying a moment of eternal youth while facing his son at the plate.

These inexplicable forces run through other pieces, too. At the heart of W. P. Kinsella's *Shoeless Joe* (you may know it as the film *Field of Dreams*) is a story of a son trying to reach his father. And Ann Hood discovers a connection she never knew.

Here one finds one source of baseball's powerful attraction: the social bonds it creates and reveals.

97

Connecting generations

"Age is a question
of mind over matter.
If you don't mind,
it doesn't matter."

—SATCHEL PAIGE

A Tough Call by Norman Rockwell, 1949.

Mark, Summer of 1994 by Kelly LaDuke, 1994.

From

Baseball and
the Meaning of Life

◆

DONALD HALL

BASEBALL CONNECTS AMERICAN MALES with each other, not only through bleacher friendships and neighbor loyalties, not only through barroom fights, but most importantly through generations. When you are small you may not discuss politics or union dues or profit margins with your father's cigar-smoking friends when your father has gone out for a six-pack; but you may discuss baseball. It is all you have in common, because your father's friend does not wish to discuss the Assistant Principal or Alice Bisbee Morgan. About the season's moment you know as much as he does; both of you may shake your heads over Lefty's wildness or the rookie who was called out last Saturday when he tried to steal home with two out in the ninth inning down by one. ❖

From
Home Game

◆

DON JOHNSON

Heat lightning silhouettes the hills
beyond the worn-out pasture
where I lob slow pitches toward a flat rock
that no longer gleams like the white rubber plate
of the majors. My father taps soft liners

to my son. Professionally crouched
over burdocks, poised above the looped runners
of morning glories, the boy breaks
with each ring of the new metal bat, stumbles
through sedge and almost catches everything.

Wearing my tattered glove like a badge,
he dreams fences for the open field,
rags the old man to hit the long ball
he could climb the wall for like Yastrzemski.
He is out there where I have been

in the child's sweatless world of fame,
but I would have changed that thunder
building on the river to the first murmur
of applause that lived already as a faint twitch
troubling the sleep of boys throughout Virginia.

Night Baseball 3 by Charles Hobson, 1989.

Memoir

◆

ANN HOOD

BASEBALL IS IN MY BLOOD. Like the light hair and eyes I inherited from my father, and the hot Italian temper I got from my mother, a love of baseball runs through my veins. Until recently, I was not sure where my passion for the sport came from. Sometimes I thought it began long ago, on summer trips to Fenway Park, when my family would drive in our oversized Chevy to Boston, park in a garage near Government Center, and take the T out to the ballpark.

As I grew older and more accustomed to our routine, my father's neatly arranged exact subway fare used to annoy me. In his pocket, I knew, he carried small bills to pay for hot dogs and beer and a souvenir program. In his wallet he had the exact amount needed to retrieve the car at day's end. What about the unknown? I used to think. But for us, that lay in the game itself. The great catch by Carlton Fisk. The Yaz home run. The pitching of Luis Tiant and Bill Lee.

Classic Fenway Clout by Bill Purdom, 1991.

It was around that same time, when my father's proclivity for careful planning bothered me, that I fell in love with the Red Sox third baseman. He was blond and blue-eyed, Number 8. I used to watch, awestruck, as he ran for balls. Once I saw him race into the dugout and emerge, arm raised high, fist clutching the baseball for an out. On our way home from games, as my father drove exactly 55, I lounged in the back seat and recalled Butch Hobson at bat, or running the bases.

In college, I dragged friends to shopping malls when he made appearances. There I would stand, in a crowd of ten-year-old boys, at Lincoln Mall, waiting for a closer look at Butch and an 8-by-10 signed photo. That photo still sits in my parents' garage, pressed into a scrapbook, surrounded by movie ticket stubs and matchbook covers and dried corsages from boys now forgotten. Sometimes I even gave Butch Hobson credit for my love of baseball.

I moved to New York City on an early summer day in 1983. It was, I remember, a perfect day for baseball. I like to think I went right then out to a ballpark, but I know this is not true. My first trip was a few days later, out to Yankee Stadium, where I was yelled at for rooting against the home team. But how could a girl from Rhode Island, a loyal Red Sox fan, become a Yankees fan? Impossible.

Like my need for a good book beside my bed, and coffee in the morning, I need baseball. So the next time the need to see a game struck me that first summer here, I boarded the number 7 train for Shea Stadium, where a young Mets team was just being formed. Butch Hobson had long ago left Boston; my heart was free. I developed a crush on the Mets' catcher, Gary Carter. I had a new apartment in a new city, a boyfriend who, in a certain light, even resembled Carter, and a baseball stadium just a subway ride away. I had found my home away from home.

Last year I won a bet. A man at a wedding I attended bet me I couldn't name the entire 1976 Red Sox team. It was a foolish bet. I had already won three margaritas from him on Mets stats.

"I know baseball," I warned him.

"Sure," he said. "Sure, you do. *Anybody* can know about the Mets. All you have to do is read the paper. But the Red Sox? 1976? Forget it."

I took a breath and began. "Yaz played first that year," I told him.

He narrowed his eyes.

I continued. The names sounded almost magical. As I recited them, I remembered those trips to Fenway Park, when a ride on the T from Government Center seemed brave and exciting. "Dwight Evans," I said, like a special incantation. "Jim Rice. Fred Lynn."

The man cleared his throat. He looked at his friend. "I've never seen a girl who knows baseball like this," he said. Then he looked at me. "Third base," he said.

I smiled. "Third base," I repeated, and imagined a long ago summer when my heart soared as I watched Number 8 leap into the dugout and emerge victorious. "Third base was Butch Hobson," I said, and collected my win.

"How did you get to be such a baseball fan?" the man said, shaking his head.

Even then I did not know that it was genetic, inherited from a woman I never got to know. That day I just shrugged and said, "I love the game. That's all."

Last year I found Butch Hobson again. My father called and told me he was managing the Pawtucket Red Sox. "Remember what a crush you had on him?" He sent me clippings from the sports pages of the *Journal*, inky arrows pointing to Butch.

When he was named the new manager of the Red Sox, my father called to tell me. "Maybe you'll come back where you belong," he said. "A Red Sox fan again."

That's when I asked him, Did he remember when my love of baseball began?

He didn't. Instead, he told me this: "My mother," he said, "loved the Cincinnati Reds. Listened to every game on the radio. The saddest day in our house was when the catcher blew the World Series, went back to his hotel room, and killed himself. I'll never forget that. I was just a kid. It was the early thirties and my mother cried when she heard the news."

I never knew my father's mother. In old faded photographs she looks back at me like a stranger. Now I know she isn't. It is because of her that baseball is in my blood. Like most things, it was passed on to me, the way these days, when I leave my apartment to catch the number 7 train to Shea Stadium, I have in my pocket exactly enough change for two subway tokens, one to get me to the game, and the other to take me back home. ❖

[OPPOSITE]
Katie Casey
by Jon Lezinsky, 1995.

Poem for My Father

for Quincy T. Trouppe, Sr.

◆

QUINCY TROUPE

father, it was an honor to be there, in the dugout with you

the glory of great black men swinging their lives as bats

at tiny white balls burning in at unbelievable speeds

riding up & in & out

a curve breaking down wicked, like a ball falling off a high table

moving away, snaking down, screwing its stitched magic

into chitling circuit air, its comma seams spinning

toward breakdown, dipping, like a hipster

bebopping a knee-dip stride in the charlie parker forties

wrist curling, like a swan's neck

behind a slick black back

cupping an invisible ball of dreams

& you there, father, regal as african obeah man

sculpted out of wood, from a sacred tree of no name no place origin

thick roots branching down into cherokee & someplace else lost

way back in africa, the sap running dry crossing

from north carolina into georgia, inside grandmother mary's womb

who was your mother & had you there in the violence of that red soil

ink blotter news gone now into blood & bone graves

of american blues, sponging rococo

truth long gone as dinosaurs
the agent-oranged landscape of former names
absent of african polysyllables, dry husk consonants there now
in their place, names flat as polluted rivers
& that guitar string smile always snaking across
some virulent american redneck's face
scorching, like atomic heat, mushrooming over nagasaki
& hiroshima, the fever-blistered shadows of it all
inked, as body etchings, into sizzled concrete
but you there, father, through it all, a yardbird solo
riffing on bat & ball glory, breaking down all fabricated myths
of white major-league legends, of who was better than who
beating them at their own crap game with killer bats
as bud powell swung his silence into beauty
of a josh gibson home run skittering across piano keys of bleachers
shattering all manufactured legends up there in lights, struck out
white knights on the risky slippery edge of amazement
awe, the miraculous truth slipping through
steeped & disguised in the blues, confluencing
like the point at the cross
when a fastball hides itself up in a shimmying slider
curve breaking down & away in a wicked sly grin
curved & broken-down like the back of an ass-scratching uncle tom
who like old satchel paige delivering his famed hesitation pitch

before coming back with a high hard fast one, rising
is sometimes slicker, slipping & sliding
& quicker than a professional hitman—

the deadliness of it all, the sudden strike
like that of the brown bomber's short crossing right
or the hook of sugar ray robinson's lightning cobra bite

& you there father through it all, catching rhythms of chono
pozo balls, drumming like cuban conga beats into your catcher's mitt
hard & fast as cool papa bell jumping into bed
before the lights went out

of the old negro baseball league, a promise you were
father, a harbinger, of shock waves, soon come

110

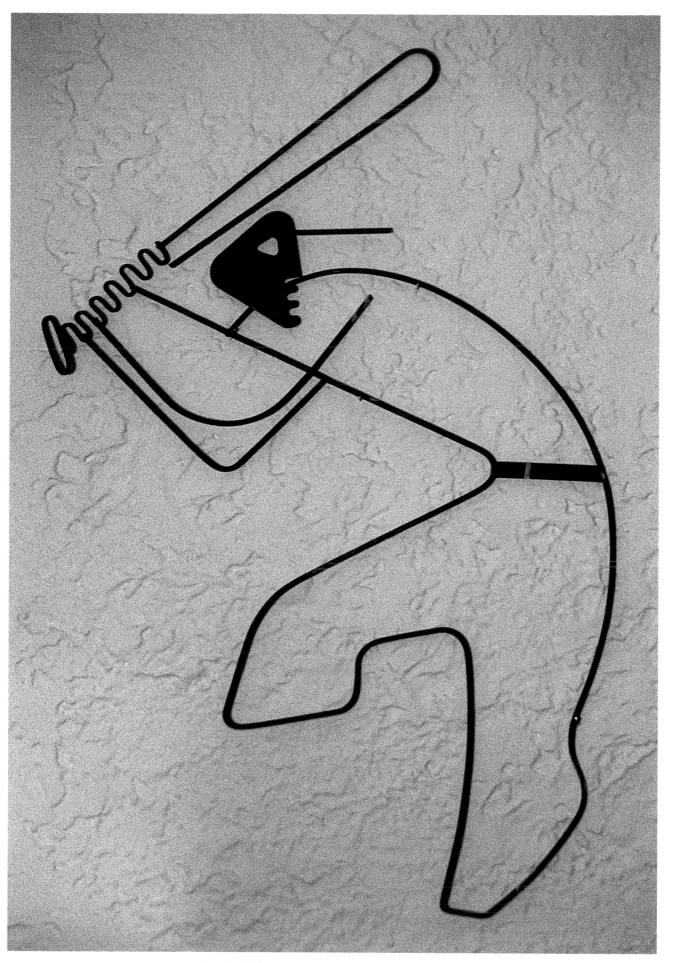

Baseball Player by Frederick Weinberg, ca. 1950.

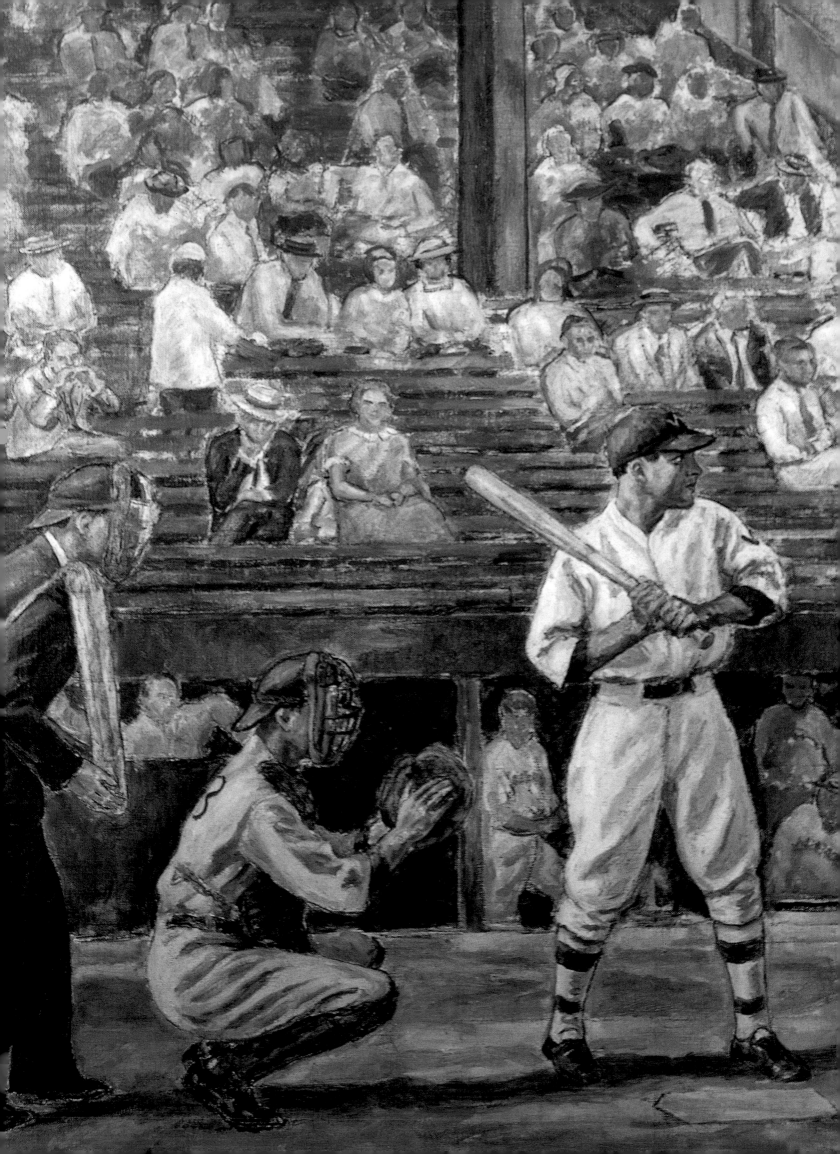

[OPPOSITE]
Detail from *Waiting for the Pitch*
by Marjorie Phillips, ca. 1939–40.

Coming to the Plate

◆

MOLLY O'NEILL

OCTOBER 16, 1990—When Paul O'Neill steps to the plate for the Cincinnati Reds tonight, he will embody the hopes of most of the 52,000 fans at Riverfront Stadium and, for at least one pitch, he will be the focal point of over 50 million televisions across America. He will also be at the center of our family's field of dreams. Since 1928, when our father, a former minor league pitcher, began throwing screwballs on his family's farm, the Series has been our manifest destiny. Baseball kept our father alive.

Tonight will be Paul's first official World Series appearance. But it isn't his first World Series experience. He has been playing baseball as if his life depended on it since he was two years old. He had to. His four older brothers would have used him as a base if he hadn't learned how to swing a bat. In addition, our father had quite a lot on his mind—a baseball career that ended in a World War II paratrooping accident, a dicey ditch-digging business, six children and an achieving wife— and he never seemed to remember any of his sons' names until he heard them announced over the public address system at the Little League park.

For ten years, my mother said, her sons seemed like an endless progression of different-colored flannel uniforms that needed to be washed. My brothers were all baseball stars. It was the roll of some very large cosmic dice that kept Paul playing the game. Two others were scouted and chose early retirement over the major leagues. One became a poet; another grew his hair long and became an entrepreneur. We all knew the consequences of these acts. "I could end up T. S. Eliot and Michael could be Donald Trump," my brother Robert said last week. "For Dad, it wouldn't come close to what Paul's doing."

We grew up in Columbus, Ohio. In a neighborhood where most children grew up Lutheran or Methodist, we grew up Baseball. It is a way of life that is as whimsical and superstitious as any other religion. Our neighbors, who were primarily academics from Ohio State University, weren't always tolerant of our rituals. The ecstasy of winning a round of home run derby by slamming a tennis ball over the fence that divided our dusty backyard from the manicured lawn next door completely escaped Mr. Walter, the owner of the manicured lawn.

His complaints ignited a slow-seething battle between my parents. To my mother, who was loath to offend, the solution was obvious: stop hitting balls. "Children can read," she would proclaim. "Children can take music lessons or ballet lessons." This irreverence astounded my father, who also didn't understand why parking his backhoe in the driveway embarrassed my mother. While they battled, a steady stream of balls continued to sail over the fence.

Mr. Walter, a soft-spoken widower, decided that we were incorrigible and spent the afternoons huddled on his back porch holding a rosary. When the ball hit the plywood backstop, he would pass a bead. When it smacked off the bat, he prayed harder. When a ball passed over the fence, he dropped his rosary, retrieved the offending sphere and retired it to his house. He thought that we possessed an inexhaustible supply of balls. He was wrong. On a given afternoon, we might run out of tennis balls but there were soft balls, hard balls, whiffle balls, soccer balls, Nerf balls, kick balls . . .

We moved away from that neighborhood when Paul was six years old. On moving day, Mr. Walter delivered hundreds of different balls, all neatly packaged in oversized cardboard storage boxes. It was his offering: his prayers had been answered. I was 15, had retired from softball three years before, and it seemed like providence that I would have my own bedroom where I could scribble deep and meaningful poetry in my diary and listen to top 40 music. My brothers were jubilant because the new house was set in the middle of four acres of potential baseball diamond.

By that time, they were a team. They had begun a ten-year reign over Central-Ohio Little League. Cincinnati had the Big Red Machine; Columbus had the O'Neill Boys. My oldest brother, Michael, was 13 and had an 80-mile-an-hour fastball. My brother Pat, who was 11, had a mean curveball. Kevin was a catcher. Robert was a pitcher. My father was the Little League coach. Paul wanted to play but he was too young for anything more than the backyard games.

The backyard games had become very serious. My brothers weren't just a team, they were a franchise. They built a baseball diamond and worked as the grounds crew to keep the infield grass groomed. They acted as park security and cleared the clubhouse, which in off-

game times doubled as a shed for our pony, Tonka. As players, they only appeared in full equipment. They looked like miniature major leaguers, so many sawed-off chess pieces in a game that began before any of us were born.

We all knew that some day we would play the game for real. It just took a couple of decades to figure out the positions we would play.

A lot of the figuring occurred intra-brother. There was brutal competition for the mound. Winning mattered most, so the position usually belonged to Michael. Kevin, who was four years younger, was the catcher, and because Michael pitched as wild as he did fast, Kevin had a strong attachment to his face guard, chest guard, shin guards and helmet. It didn't surprise any of us when, at 13 years old, Kevin retired from baseball and started playing football. He liked the equipment.

Games of "hot box"—one player on first, another on second and a runner in between— proved that Pat, who loved the game more than any other brother, possessed the least physical gift. He is built a little too low to the ground. Robert, although five years younger, was Mike's singular competition for the mound. He pitched smart and steady. Paul was stuck with leftovers. He was just a little boy when the rest of my brothers entered adolescence, en masse. He started facing Michael when he was eight years old. The others were sick of being hit by pitches. Paul took any pitches he could get.

His earliest training as a competitor was as a sort of pillow for his older brothers' Gestalt therapy. In the years when Robert fought to unseat Michael on the pitcher's mound, he relaxed by challenging Paul to 25-point games of one-on-one basketball. Coolly, Robert would allow a 23-point lead. And then, with the same dramatic effortlessness every afternoon, Robert would take the next 25 points from Paul.

The game never changed, and neither did Paul's reaction. "You cheater," he would shriek, hurling the basketball and storming into the house to call our mother at the hospital where she worked. "Mom," he would sob into the phone, after our mother had been paged from a death bed or an emergency room, "Robert cheated."

Paul had a sense of injustice early on. He criminalized his individual tormentors. If an older brother was in the process of winning, he was "lucky." If he won, he had "cheated," and Paul would follow the sinner around with challenges for rematches phrased in a sportsmanlike manner: "What's the matter, cheater? Afraid you won't get lucky again?" My father interceded occasionally. "Quit torturing the darned baby, will ya?" he'd say.

Although usually, a game was a game in our house, a winner was a winner and only losers needed umpires. During his early childhood, the injustice for Paul was birth order: In the end, it may have been a lucky break. He was two years old when the older boys began to dominate Plain City.

Cincinnati had Crosley Field; Ohio Little League had Plain City. It was a Little League-scale replica of a major league park in an Amish community 25 miles northwest of Columbus. Plain City had a grass infield, dugouts and uniformed umpires. It had a scoreboard, a concessions stand and stadium-style stands. The Plain City games were our World Series. My father, the coach, would sit on the bench chewing like Don Zimmer. My brothers would play out their Catfish Hunter fantasies.

My mother and I would sit in the stands with Paul. He wore little sunsuits and I remember the way his blond curls smelled, the way the mosquitoes buzzed around us on those muggy Midwestern summer evenings. My attendance was mandatory, I was furious and bored and carried books like Sylvia Plath's *Bell Jar* to read during the game. But Paul, from whom I was inseparable for the first eight years of his life, kept me connected to the game.

There was a dirt race track surrounding the Plain City ball park and one night an Amish man steered his horse and buggy around the track during the bottom of the sixth and final inning. In his Abraham Lincoln hat and top coat, the buggy driver looked like something out of a 19th-century museum. Michael was playing right field in that game. His team was one run up, with a runner on base and two out, when a routine fly ball landed at his feet. He was watching the horse and buggy. "He missed the ball, Ollee," Paul said, his earliest and enduring pronunciation of my name recalling the boxer Muhammed Ali. "Tell him to get it," he screamed.

He was too old to sit on my lap when Robert began pitching. If he had persevered, I suppose Robert would have been a reliever. He'd do anything to prevent a batter getting ahead of him. If they did, he collapsed. In one tied game at Plain City, with the bases loaded on walks and a full count, he began sobbing into the mitt on his left hand and consoling himself with his right hand, which was slipped down the front of his flannel green and white pinstriped pants. "My god," whispered our horrified mother.

Maybe Paul learned from his older brothers' mistakes; he certainly learned the symmetry between baseball and life. Like the rest of us, he wasn't surprised when Robert, who was already being looked at by major league scouts, retired from baseball at age 15 and took up poetry and tennis. Even more than batters getting ahead of him, Robert loathed fielders who blew the play on a perfect groundball pitch.

He is the only brother who believes that he might have made a mistake about baseball. When Paul negotiates his contract, Robert, who is now 30 years old and weighs 220 pounds, is quick to point out that he, not Paul, was the m.v.p. of Plain City. "It's on the records," he says. "M.v.p. 1972. Paul only got most valuable pitcher and that was in 1974."

In a reversal of their one-on-one games, Robert calls Paul "lucky." "He's the only one who could go to the Ohio State Fair and blow the balloon off the clown's mouth and come home with all the prizes," he says.

Paul's luck went as unnoticed as his performance on the Little League field did. A few years later, when he broke his ankle sliding into second base in Plain City, nobody thought it was a big deal that he played right field in a cast and led the team in batting. That's what O'Neill Boys do.

Besides, the world had started to change. As an all-city high school player, Michael was engaged in a haircut battle. Today, he says that it was symptomatic of his "uncoachableness." Then, he said, "What difference does it make how long my hair is if I am blowing away the batters?" Scouts still watched him, but he realized that his career potential was limited during his first year of college. "During a game after a particularly rough fraternity party," he told me yesterday, "I saw three balls coming at me instead of one."

Something similar happened to Pat in his senior year of high school. He quit baseball so that he could work in a grocery store and buy a car.

Paul was too young to drive a car or suffer the long-reaching ripples of Woodstock nation that washed over the rest of our adolescence. He kept playing baseball. My father, his top four prospects benched for life, focused exclusively on Paul. He called his youngest son "Mike, Pat, Kev or Rob, no, Paul." By the time he was in high school, Paul was the only one living at home. The rest of us were being socially relevant in places like Haight Ashbury and Provincetown.

Paul was at home when our parents began to look older. He called our father Little Buddy, and Old Timer. In 1980, when the telephone rang in our parents' kitchen with the news that Paul was Cincinnati's fourth-round draft pick, the Old Timer cried.

Nobody else was surprised. Nevertheless, the process of Paul's career pulled us back together, back into the story of our childhood, complete with the unresolved challenges and the echoes of "Cheater!" and "Luck!"

As Paul moved between single, double and triple A baseball, our other brothers drifted between careers. I suppose they tended some demons and doubt. Nobody talked about it. Everybody rooted for Paul. But since we grew up in the church of Baseball, we know why our father has outlived four of his brothers, we know what kept him alive during emergency bypass surgery the year that Paul moved up to the majors, we know about teams, we know for what we cheer.

None of it surprises us. Last week, sitting in a Broadway theater, in the middle of the second act of *Lettice and Lovage*, I had an irrepressible urge to put on my Walkman, which was tuned to WFAN. Paul had called me from the locker room before the game; I just had this feeling. I tuned in to an announcer yelling, "It's over the right field fence! A home run for O'Neill." My companion was amazed. I wasn't surprised.

Several nights later, I was watching the game on television when the Reds clinched the pennant. A few minutes passed before my brother Robert called. He was watching the post-game shows at his home in Cincinnati. "I haven't seen Paul on the screen," he said. "I have this feeling he's standing by his locker, waiting for somebody to come and tell him he's the m.v.p." We listened to each other breathe and listened as our separate televisions announced that two relief pitchers had been named joint m.v.p.'s.

"Oh, man," said Robert, "OK, look. I have this big pumpkin, OK? It's going to say 'REDS' in big victorious letters and I am going to put a candle in it and I'm going to take it over and put it on Paul's front porch before he gets home. He'll spend the whole night trying to figure out who did it. It might give him a laugh. He might think it's lucky."

After a pause, my brother Robert continued his declaration of full adulthood. "Look I gotta go, OK?" he said. "See you at the game on Tuesday. Wear red." ❖

[OPPOSITE]
Big Leaguer book cover, 1920s.

[FOLLOWING PAGES]
Night Baseball by Marjorie Phillips, 1951.
The Phillips Collection, Washington, D.C.

Striking Out My Son
in the Father-Son Game

◆

RON SMITH

Caught in the open in broad daylight,
jerky-eyed with doubt,
he swings like someone
who's never held a bat.

His elbows wrongly angle in,
his wrists are snapless
when the soft, lopsided sphere
drops from the sky.

Anyway, those wobbly ankles
and rattly knees cannot
spank those Nikes off the bases
or make a proper feet-first slide.

His eyes are everywhere
but on the ball. I arc
three adequate pitches
and retire the side.

We joke our stiff adult jokes
to the plate and cock
our clubs at our squawking,
crouching sons.

Despite the jolt to dozing muscles,
we find we can still hit
and run. Bellies leaning
toward the outfield,

we circle and circle the bags.
On the mound a grim boy tiptoes
to see his best pitch ride
into the left field pines.

Another banker scores.
My son slinks among a dozen fielders,
trying to hide.
He will have to come

to the plate again
with that gap between his fists
I haven't made him close.
I climb the red clay,

toe the rubber, and spit.
From a row of hooting women
My wife glares at me
through the shimmer of heat.

She can see the blood in my face
that means the steeper drop,
the slow backspin. These little boys
will never hit me today.

120

[OPPOSITE]
Baseball Player
by Steven Skollar, 1997.

THE CYCLE

From
Snow in August

◆

PETE HAMILL

ON THE LAST TUESDAY IN JUNE, with the sun high in the Brooklyn sky and a clean breeze blowing from the harbor, they went together to Ebbets Field. They met at the entrance to Prospect Park, the rabbi in his black suit, black hat, and white socks, Michael in gabardine slacks and a windbreaker. The boy made good speed on his crutches. His face was no longer black and swollen, but there were still purple smudges under his eyes and his ribs hurt when he laughed. In the pockets of the windbreaker he carried cheese sandwiches prepared by his mother.

"We should take a taxi," the rabbi said.

"It costs too much, Rabbi," Michael said. "Besides, I'm getting pretty good with these things. And I need the exercise."

Outside Ebbets Field **by William Feldman, 1994.**

As they crossed a transverse road into the Big Meadow, he gazed from a hill upon the long lines of fans coming across the swards of summer green. Kids and grown-ups, grown-ups and kids, in groups of six or seven, but following each other in a steady movement, carrying bags of food and cases of beer and soda. He and the rabbi moved to join the long lines, the rubber tips of Michael's crutches digging into the grass, slowing him down. Some fans wore Dodger caps and T-shirts, others wore the clothes of workingmen. Some carried portable radios, and music echoed through the great meadow, bouncing off the hill where the Quaker cemetery had been since before the American Revolution. Michael told the rabbi that George Washington had retreated across this park after losing the Battle of Long Island, and the rabbi looked around alertly, as if remembering other hills and other retreats.

The smaller groups came together at the path that snaked around past the Swan Lake. The voices were abruptly louder in the narrow space, the music clashing and then blending like the sound of a carnival. They went past Devil's Cave and over a stone bridge, with the zoo to the left, another lake to the right, the trees higher, the earth darker. There were no signs giving directions, but they were not needed; everybody knew the way to Ebbets Field.

"In the legs, you will have big muscles, like a soccer player," the rabbi said, as they reached another roadway through the park and followed the thickening crowd.

"I never played soccer," Michael said. "Did you?"

"In secret," the rabbi confided. "My father worried too much, and then my secret he discovered. He stopped me."

He sighed and shook his head.

"My father said Jews don't play soccer, and rabbis never!" he explained. "Maybe he was right. I don't think so."

Then other lines of people were joining the throng, men and boys and a few women from other parts of Brooklyn, converging like pilgrims coming to a shrine.

"I love America!" Rabbi Hirsch suddenly exclaimed.

Michael smiled.

"Look at it! All around is America! You see it? Crazy people coming for the baseball, for the bunts and the triples and the rhubarbs! Look: Irish and Jews and Italians and Spanish, every kind of people. Poles too! I hear them talking. Listen: words from every place. From all countries! Coming to Abbot's Field!"

"*Ebbets* Field," Michael said.

"That's what I said. Abbot's Field! Look at the fanatics, boychik. Up in the morning with nothing to do except see the baseball? What a country."

"Well, school is out and—"

"But the men! Look at the men! On a *Tuesday*! How can they not work? In every country, on a Tuesday, you work!"

"Maybe they work nights. Maybe they're on vacation."

"No. No, it's—they are *Americans*."

The rabbi was inhaling deeply as he walked and talked, as if memorizing the odors of the brilliant Tuesday morning. He was free of the closed air of the synagogue basement, and he loved it. He was perspiring heavily in his black suit, wiping away sweat with a finger, stopping to drink from a stone water fountain. But his body seemed oddly lighter, and he walked with a joyous bounce.

And then up ahead, through two stone pillars, the trees vanished and the light was brighter, and they could smell hot dogs frying and hear car horns honking. They were pulled along in the human river, out of the park and into Flatbush Avenue. Now another great human stream was feeding the river, a darker stream, as hundreds of Negroes arrived, many of them with gray hair and paunchy bodies and lined faces. They were walking from Bedford-Stuyvesant. They were coming from the Franklin Avenue stop of the IRT. They were hopping off buses. The older ones had waited decade after decade for a morning like this. They had waited for longer than Michael had been alive.

And he gazed at them, more Negroes than he had ever seen before, some of them coal-colored and some chocolate-colored and others with skin the color of tea with milk. There were flat-faced Negroes and hawk-nosed Negroes, men with wide eyes and squinty eyes, fat men and skinny no-assed men, men who looked like prizefighters and men who looked like professors. All greeting each other with jokes and smiles and handshakes.

"America!" the rabbi said. "What a place."

And then before them, rising above the low houses, above the umbrellas of the hot dog carts and the whorls of cotton candy, right there in front of them was Ebbets Field. Up there was the magnet pulling all of them through the summer morning. Up there was Jackie Robinson.

Michael felt unreal as he moved with the rabbi through the crowd. The scene was like Coney Island and the circus and the day the war ended, all in one. And Michael was in it, part of it, feeding it. Music blared from the concession stands. Men with aprons and change machines hawked programs and pictures of the Dodgers, pennants and posters. A grouchy woman stood beside a cloth-covered board that was jammed with buttons. All were selling for 25 cents.

"Pick one!" the rabbi said.

Michael chose a button that said I'M FOR JACKIE.

"Two!" said the rabbi.

They moved on, their buttons pinned above their hearts. They eased along Sullivan Street, staring up at the weather-stained facade of the great ballpark. It was more beautiful and immense than anything Michael had ever seen. Bigger than any building in the parish. Bigger than any church. He paused, balanced on the crutches, to allow the sight to fill him. So did the rabbi. They stared up at the structure, seeing people walking up ramps, and behind them, thick slashing bars of black girders and patches of blue sky through the bars. As they stood there, like pilgrims, the crowd eddied around them, and Michael felt a tingle that was like that moment in a solemn high mass when the priests would sing a Gregorian chant and the altar seemed to glow with mystery.

Then they turned another corner, into Montgomery Street, and found one more entrance, *their* entrance, and a guy bellowing, "Program, getcha program here!" The rabbi pushed his glasses up on his brow and squinted at their tickets.

"This is the hard part," he said. "To find the chairs."

"Seats, Rabbi."

"Here, you look."

Michael examined the tickets and led the way to the gate. A gray little man with a mashed nose like a prizefighter's was guarding the turnstile. Rabbi Hirsch handed him the tickets and he tore them in half and gave back the stubs.

"Enjoy da game, Rabbi," the ticket taker said brusquely.

The rabbi looked startled.

"Enjoy da game," he said to himself, passing through the turnstile after Michael, shaking his head in wonder. America.

Inside, Michael stood under the stands, not moving for a long moment. Savoring it. Inhaling the cool smell of unseen earth and grass. Feeling holy.

I am here, he thought, in Ebbets Field. At last.

Then they climbed and climbed on the ramps, the crutch pads digging into Michael's armpits, the dank, shadowed air smelling now of concrete and old iron, ushers directing them ever onward, climbing until the street seemed far below them and Michael could see the church steeples scattered across the endless distances of Brooklyn. The crowds thinned. Then they passed through a final darkness. And Michael could feel his stomach move up and then down and his heart stood still.

For there it was. Below them and around them. Greener than any place he had ever seen. There was the tan diamond of his imagination. There were the white foul lines as if cut with a razor through a painting. There were the dugouts. And the stands. And most beautiful of all, there below him, the green grass of Ebbets Field.

Ballplayers were lolling in the grass, tossing balls back and forth, breaking into sudden sprints. They were directly beneath him and the rabbi. The Pirates. The rabbi gripped a railing for a moment, as if afraid of losing his balance and tumbling down the steps and out onto the field.

"Is very high," he said, his face dubious.

But an usher directed them to their section, and they found their seats, on the aisle, eight rows up in left-center field. The rabbi sat in the end seat. The seats beside Michael were empty. Behind them were three men wearing caps adorned with union buttons. International Longshoremen of America. Michael explained to Rabbi Hirsch that the game hadn't yet begun, that the Pittsburgh players were taking batting practice, getting ready for the game. Together, as they ate Kate Devlin's cheese sandwiches, Michael and the rabbi, like new arrivals in Heaven, explored the geography of the field. They could see the famous concave wall in right field and the screen towering forty feet above it, with Bedford Avenue beyond. Red Barber had helped put that screen into their imaginations, and there it was before them, as real as breakfast.

"An Old Goldie you could hit over the fence?" the rabbi said.

Michael said Yes, over the fence was an Old Goldie. He showed the rabbi the famous sign in center field where Abe Stark of Pitkin Avenue promised a suit to any player who hit it with a fly ball. "A heart attack the fielder would need to have for a ball to hit this sign," the rabbi said, and Michael laughed. There were other signs too, for Bulova watches and Van Heusen shirts, for Gem razor blades and Winthrop shoes, but Abe Stark's sign was the only one anybody ever remembered. Michael explained the distances marked on the walls: 297 feet to right field, 405 feet to center, 343 to left. He explained the scoreboard. He explained the dugouts. He was explaining the pitcher's mound, and its height, and the meaning of the word *mound*, when there was a sudden sharp crack and a ball sailed from distant home plate on a high, deep line to the upper deck in left field.

Then another crack, another ball flying into the upper deck while the crowd ooohed.

Then another.

"Jesus, that Kiner kid can hit the baseball, all right," a man behind them growled.

"No doubt about it, Louis," his friend said.

"Even if it's on'y battin' practice."

"He does it in games too, this guy."

Ralph Kiner! A rookie last year, out of the navy. Now the big young star of the Pirates. Driving one ball after another into the stands. At the lowest point, the drive went 343 feet; balls hit into the upper deck would go 450 feet. Michael was afraid for a moment, imagining Kiner doing it in the game to Ralph Branca, the Dodger pitcher. On this day, the Dodgers must win; he did not want to remember forever a Dodger defeat. Then he thought: The man's right, it's only batting practice.

Then Kiner was finished and behind him came another batter. There was a medium-sized cheer, and the rabbi asked why in Brooklyn they were cheering for a player from Pittsburgh. The growling man behind them gave the explanation.

[OPPOSITE]
Detail from
Sunlit Ebbets Field
by William Feldman, 1987.

Hank Greenberg
by **Jeffrey Rubin, 1995.**

"Here's Greenboig," he said.

And Michael then told the rabbi about Hank Greenberg, who spent all of his life with the Tigers in Detroit and was one of the greatest of all hitters. One year he hit 58 home runs, only 2 less than Babe Ruth's 60. Michael didn't know as much about the American League as he did about the National, but he knew these things from reading the newspapers, and he explained that Greenberg had been in the air corps out in India or someplace and this was his first year in the National League and might be his last.

"Okay, this I understand," the rabbi said, rising slowly to gaze across the field at the tiny, distant figure of Hank Greenberg. The rabbi stood so proudly that Michael thought he was going to salute. Greenberg lined two balls against the left-field wall. He hit two towering pop-ups. Then, as the rabbi sat down, he hit a long fly ball to center. The Pittsburgh outfielders watched it, tensed, then saw where it was going and stepped aside, doffing their caps and bowing.

The ball bounced off Abe Stark's sign.

There was a tremendous roar, with shocked pigeons rising off the roof of the ballpark, and everybody was standing and the outfielders were laughing.

"He hits the sign!" the rabbi shouted exultantly. "He wins the suit!"

The guys behind them were also laughing and discussing the sign, as batting practice ended and the Pirates trotted off the field.

"Dey can't give 'im da suit from battin' practice," one of them said.

"Wait a minnit, Jabbo, wait a minnit. Look at dat sign. Does it say, Hit Sign Win Suit, except in *battin'* practice?"

"No, but Ralph, da outfield went in da dumpeh! Dey let da ball go pas' dem! Dey di'n't even *try*."

"I say Greenboig gets da suit, whatta ya bet?" said the one named Louis.

The debate was erased by another roar, as the Dodgers took the field and everyone in Ebbets Field stood to cheer. Two Negro men arrived at their aisle, carrying programs. One was very dark and wore a Dodger cap. The other was pale-skinned and wore a Hawaiian shirt and had field glasses hanging from his neck.

"Scuse me, pardon us," said the man in the Dodger cap. They were in the third and fourth seats. The one with the field glasses sat beside Michael. He glanced at the I'M FOR JACKIE button and smiled.

"Great day for baseball," he said.

"Sure is," Michael said.

"Enjoy da game," Rabbi Hirsch said.

A group of young men came up the aisle, laughing, posing, about six of them, and took seats across the aisle on the right, a few rows higher than Michael and the rabbi. They wore T-shirts with the sleeves rolled up over their shoulders and tight pegged pants. None of them wore a hat, and their Vaselined hair glistened in the light. They were all smoking cigarettes, and one held a pint bottle in a paper bag. They reminded Michael of the Falcons.

For a moment he felt a coil of fear in his stomach. But he turned away and gazed down at the field. This was Ebbets Field in broad daylight, not a dark street beside the factory. The Dodgers ambled to their positions. And Holy God, there was Pete Reiser! Going out to left field! Back from the dead. Furillo was in center and Gene Hermanski in right. But Pistol Pete Reiser was with them, down there on the grass. Michael pointed him out to Rabbi Hirsch.

"He looks okay, boychik," the rabbi said. "Maybe some prayers helped. And maybe some hits he'll get." ❖

Behind a Ballfield by Stephen Fox, 1999.

The Kid

◆

E. ETHELBERT MILLER

about the second month of the season
we start catching word about the kid
talk about strikeouts and shutouts
how his curve breaks and his fastball smokes
frank and i were driving trucks up in the mountains
listening to the games
betting our wages and drinking beer
we get the newspapers each morning and check the standings
frank is a giants fan
been that way since the day willie mays broke in
that was the same year his father died
in an accident on the highway three days before christmas
sometimes when we ain't talking about baseball
frank will talk about his father
talk about him the way some folks be talking about the kid

poem for my 71st birthday

◆

CHARLES BUKOWSKI

yes, I'm still here, doing about what I've always
done, although there are some moments of
hesitation
like I'll be at the plate and the big guy out
there will be about ready to fire one in
and I'll call time, step outside the batter's
box, knock some dirt off my cleats, look
around, there are sometimes blinding flashes of
light in my eyes
but I'll gather myself, shake it off, get back
in the box, feel the power returning, I
can't wait for the big guy's next pitch and it
comes in, a slider, bastard can't fool me,
I get the wood on it, it goes out of there,
way out of there and I trot the bases
as the young guys curse me under their
breath; too bad fellows, you see you
have to have a feel for it and as long as
it's there, you keep going, and when
you can't do it anymore, you'll still be
asking for one more turn at bat, just to
be there, even to swing and miss, it's the
doing that gets it done,
don't you understand this?

like this one here, it's probably only
a single or a short hopper to the
shortstop,
but I've had my swing
and I'll be back a few times
more,
the big guy doesn't have me
out of here
yet.

Honus Wagner by Charles Martin Conlon, 1912.

From
Shoeless Joe

◆

W. P. KINSELLA

MY FATHER SAID HE SAW HIM years later playing in a tenth-rate commercial league in a textile town in Carolina, wearing shoes and an assumed name.

"He'd put on fifty pounds and the spring was gone from his step in the outfield, but he could still hit. Oh, how that man could hit. No one has ever been able to hit like Shoeless Joe."

Three years ago at dusk on a spring evening, when the sky was a robin's-egg blue and the wind as soft as a day-old chick, I was sitting on the verandah of my farm home in eastern Iowa when a voice very clearly said to me, "If you build it, he will come."

Shoeless Joe's Last at Bat
by Thom Ross, 1989.

The voice was that of a ballpark announcer. As he spoke, I instantly envisioned the finished product I knew I was being asked to conceive. I could see the dark, squarish speakers, like ancient sailors' hats, attached to aluminum-painted light standards that glowed down into a baseball field, my present position being directly behind home plate.

In reality, all anyone else could see out there in front of me was a tattered lawn of mostly dandelions and quack grass that petered out at the edge of a cornfield perhaps fifty yards from the house.

Anyone else was my wife Annie, my daughter Karin, a corn-colored collie named Carmeletia Pope, and a cinnamon and white guinea pig named Junior who ate spaghetti and sang each time the fridge door opened. Karin and the dog were not quite two years old.

"If you build it, he will come," the announcer repeated in scratchy Middle American, as if his voice had been recorded on an old 78-r.p.m. record.

A three-hour lecture or a 500-page guide book could not have given me clearer directions: Dimensions of ballparks jumped over and around me like fleas, cost figures for light standards and floodlights whirled around my head like the moths that dusted against the porch light above me.

That was all the instruction I ever received: two announcements and a vision of a baseball field. I sat on the verandah until the satiny dark was complete. A few curdly clouds striped the moon, and it became so silent I could hear my eyes blink.

Our house is one of those massive old farm homes, square as a biscuit box with a sagging verandah on three sides. The floor of the verandah slopes so that marbles, baseballs, tennis balls, and ball bearings all accumulate in a corner like a herd of cattle clustered with their backs to a storm. On the north verandah is a wooden porch swing where Annie and I sit on humid August nights, sip lemonade from teary glasses, and dream.

When I finally went to bed, and after Annie inched into my arms in that way she has, like a cat that you suddenly find sound asleep in your lap, I told her about the voice and I told her that I knew what it wanted me to do.

"Oh love," she said, "if it makes you happy you should do it," and she found my lips with hers. I shivered involuntarily as her tongue touched mine.

Annie: She has never once called me crazy. Just before I started the first landscape work, as I stood looking out at the lawn and the cornfield, wondering how it could look so different in daylight, considering the notion of accepting it all as a dream and abandoning it, Annie appeared at my side and her arm circled my waist. She leaned against me and looked up, cocking her head like one of the red squirrels that scamper along the power lines from the highway to the house. "Do it, love," she said as I looked down at her, that slip of a girl with hair the color of cayenne pepper and at least a million freckles on her face and arms, that girl who lives in blue jeans and T-shirts and at twenty-four could still pass for sixteen.

I thought back to when I first knew her. I came to Iowa to study. She was the child of my landlady. I heard her one afternoon outside my window as she told her girlfriends, "When I grow up I'm going to marry . . ." and she named me. The others were going to be nurses, teachers, pilots, or movie stars, but Annie chose me as her occupation. Eight years later we were married. I chose willingly, lovingly, to stay in Iowa. Eventually I rented this farm, then bought it, operating it one inch from bankruptcy. I don't seem meant to farm, but I want to be close to this precious land, for Annie and me to be able to say, "This is ours."

Now I stand ready to cut into the cornfield, to chisel away a piece of our livelihood to use as dream currency, and Annie says, "Oh, love, if it makes you happy you should do it." I carry her words in the back of my mind, stored the way a maiden aunt might wrap a brooch, a

Joseph Jefferson Jackson
by Milo Weidemann, 1919.

remembrance of a long-lost love. I understand how hard that was for her to say and how it got harder as the project advanced. How she must have told her family not to ask me about the baseball field I was building, because they stared at me dumb-eyed, a row of silent, thickset peasants with red faces. Not an imagination among them except to forecast the wrath of God that will fall on the heads of pagans such as 1.

"If you build it, he will come."

He, of course, was Shoeless Joe Jackson.

Joseph Jefferson (Shoeless Joe) Jackson
Born: Brandon Mills, South Carolina,
    July 16, 1887
Died: Greenville, South Carolina,
    December 5, 1951

In April 1945, Ty Cobb picked Shoeless Joe as the best left fielder of all time. A famous sportswriter once called Joe's glove "the place where triples go to die." He never learned to read or write. He created legends with a bat and a glove.

Was it really a voice I heard? Or was it perhaps something inside me making a statement that I did not hear with my ears but with my heart? Why should I want to follow this command? But as I ask, I already know the answer. I count the loves in my life: Annie, Karin, Iowa, Baseball. The great god Baseball.

My birthstone is a diamond. When asked, I say my astrological sign is hit and run, which draws a lot of blank stares here in Iowa where 50,000 people go to see the University of Iowa Hawkeyes football team while 500 regulars, including me, watch the baseball team perform.

My father, I've been told, talked baseball statistics to my mother's belly while waiting for me to be born.

My father: born, Glen Ullin, North Dakota, April 14, 1896. Another diamond birthstone. Never saw a professional baseball game until

1919 when he came back from World War I where he had been gassed at Passchendaele. He settled in Chicago, inhabited a room above a bar across from Comiskey Park, and quickly learned to live and die with the White Sox. Died a little when, as prohibitive favorites, they lost the 1919 World Series to Cincinnati, died a lot the next summer when eight members of the team were accused of throwing that World Series.

Before I knew what baseball was, I knew of Connie Mack, John McGraw, Grover Cleveland Alexander, Ty Cobb, Babe Ruth, Tris Speaker, Tinker-to-Evers-to-Chance, and, of course, Shoeless Joe Jackson. My father loved underdogs, cheered for the Brooklyn Dodgers and the hapless St. Louis Browns, loathed the Yankees—an inherited trait, I believe—and insisted that Shoeless Joe was innocent, a victim of big business and crooked gamblers.

That first night, immediately after the voice and the vision, I did nothing except sip my lemonade a little faster and rattle the ice cubes in my glass. The vision of the baseball park lingered—swimming, swaying, seeming to be made of red steam, though perhaps it was only the sunset. And there was a vision within the vision: one of Shoeless Joe Jackson playing left field. Shoeless Joe Jackson who last played major league baseball in 1920 and was suspended for life, along with seven of his compatriots, by Commissioner Kenesaw Mountain Landis, for his part in throwing the 1919 World Series.

Instead of nursery rhymes, I was raised on the story of the Black Sox Scandal, and instead of Tom Thumb or Rumpelstiltskin, I grew up hearing of the eight disgraced ballplayers: Weaver, Cicotte, Risberg, Felsch, Gandil, Williams, McMullin, and, always, Shoeless Joe Jackson.

"He hit .375 against the Reds in the 1919 World Series and played errorless ball," my father would say, scratching his head in wonder. "Twelve hits in an eight-game series. And *they* suspended *him*," Father would cry. Shoeless Joe became a symbol of the tyranny of the powerful over the powerless. The name Kenesaw Mountain Landis became synonymous with the Devil.

Building a baseball field is more work than you might imagine. I laid out a whole field, but it was there in spirit only. It was really only left field that concerned me. Home plate was made from pieces of cracked two-by-four embedded in the earth. The pitcher's rubber rocked like a cradle when I stood on it. The bases were stray blocks of wood, unanchored. There was no backstop or grandstand, only one shaky bleacher beyond the left-field wall. There was a left-field wall, but only about fifty feet of it, twelve feet high, stained dark green and braced from the rear. And the left-field grass. My intuition told me that it was the grass that was important. It took me three seasons to hone that grass to its proper texture, to its proper color. I made trips to Minneapolis and one or two other cities where the stadiums still have natural-grass infields and outfields. I would arrive hours before a game and watch the groundskeepers groom the field like a prize animal, then stay after the game when in the cool of the night the same groundsmen appeared with hoses, hoes, and rakes, and patched the grasses like medics attending to wounded soldiers.

I pretended to be building a Little League ballfield and asked their secrets and sometimes was told. I took interest in the total operation; they wouldn't understand if I told them I was building only a left field.

Three seasons I've spent seeding, watering, fussing, praying, coddling that field like a sick child. Now it glows parrot-green, cool as mint, soft as moss, lying there like a cashmere blanket. I've begun watching it in the evenings, sitting on the rickety bleacher just beyond the fence. A bleacher I constructed for an audience of one. ❖

Night Game-'Tis a Bunt
by Ralph Fasanella, 1981.

From
Bull Durham

◆

RON SHELTON

ANNIE SAVOY
(Susan Sarandon)

I BELIEVE in the Church of Baseball. I've tried all the major religions, and most of the minor ones. I've worshipped Buddha, Allah, Brahma, Vishnu, Siva, trees, mushrooms, and Isadora Duncan. I know things. For instance, there are 108 beads in a Catholic rosary and there are 108 stitches in a baseball. When I heard that, I gave Jesus a chance. But it just didn't work out between us. The Lord laid too much guilt on me. I prefer metaphysics to theology. You see, there's no guilt in baseball, and it's never boring. . . . I've tried 'em all, I really have, and the only church that truly feeds the soul, day in, day out, is the Church of Baseball.

THE SATURDAY EVENING POST
An
kly
Found
anklin
Volume 204, Number 48
10c. in Canada
(INCLUDING TAX)
MAY 28, 1932
5c. THE COPY
J. F
-KERNAN-
FRANCIS HACKETT—COREY FORD—HARRY S. NEW

From
The Web of the Game

◆

ROGER ANGELL

[The New Yorker *writer Roger Angell recorded the wisdom of ninety-one-year-old Joe Wood, Red Sox fastballer of the early 1900s, as the two watched a Yale–St. John's game in New Haven in 1981.*]

OUR AFTERNOON SLID BY IN A DISTRACTION OF BASEBALL AND MEMORY, and I almost felt myself at some dreamlike doubleheader involving the then and the now—the semi-anonymous strong young men waging their close, marvelous game on the sunlit green field before us while bygone players and heroes of baseball history—long gone now, most of them—replayed their vivid, famous innings for me in the words and recollections of my companion. . . .

In the home half of the sixth, Yale put its leadoff batter aboard with a single but could not bunt him along. Joe Wood was distressed. "I could teach these fellows to bunt in one minute," he said. "Nobody can't hardly bunt anymore. You've got to get your weight more forward than he did, so you're not reaching for the ball. And he should have his right hand higher up on the bat."

The inning ended, and we reversed directions once again. "Ty Cobb was the greatest bat-handler you ever saw," Wood said. "He used to go out to the ballpark early in the morning with a pitcher and work on hitting the ball to all fields, over and over. He batted that strange way, with his fists apart, you know, but he could have hit just as well no matter how he held it. He just knew what to do with a bat in hand. And base running—why, I saw him get on base and steal second, steal third, and then steal home. *The* best. A lot of fellows in my time shortened up on the bat when they had to—that's what the St. John's boys should try against this good pitcher. Next to Cobb, Shoeless Joe Jackson was the best left-handed hitter I ever saw, and he was always down at the end of the bat until there were two strikes on him. Then he'd shorten up a little, to give himself a better chance."

Dick Lee said, "That's what you've been telling Charlie Polka, isn't it, Joe?"

"Yes, sir, and it's helped him," Wood said. "He's tried it, and now he knows that all you have to do is make contact and the ball will fly a long way."

Both men saw my look of bewilderment, and they laughed together.

"Charlie Polka is a Little League player," Dick Lee explained. "He's about eleven years old."

"He lives right across the street from me," Wood said. "He plays for the 500 Blake team—that's named for a restaurant here in town. I've got him shortened up on the bat, and now he's a hitter. Charlie Polka is a natural." ❖

141

The Green Fields of the Mind

◆

A. BARTLETT GIAMATTI

IT BREAKS YOUR HEART. It is designed to break your heart. The game begins in the spring, when everything else begins again, and it blossoms in the summer, filling the afternoons and evenings, and then as soon as the chill rains come, it stops and leaves you to face the fall alone. You count on it, rely on it to buffer the passage of time, to keep the memory of sunshine and high skies alive, and then just when the days are all twilight, when you need it most, it stops. Today, October 2, a Sunday of rain and broken branches and leaf-clogged drains and slick streets, it stopped, and summer was gone.

Somehow, the summer seemed to slip by faster this time. Maybe it wasn't this summer, but all the summers that, in this my fortieth summer, slipped by so fast. There comes a time when every summer will have something of autumn about it. Whatever the reason, it seemed to me that I was investing more and more in baseball, making the game do more of the work that keeps time fat and slow and lazy. I was counting on the game's deep patterns, three strikes, three outs, three times three innings, and its deepest impulse, to go out and back, to leave and to return home, to set the order of the day and to organize the daylight. I wrote a few things this last summer, this summer that did not last, nothing grand but some things, and yet that work was just camouflage. The real activity was

Fenway Park, Boston, MA, by **Jim Dow, 1981.**

done with the radio—not the all-seeing, all-falsifying television—and was the playing of the game in the only place it will last, the enclosed, green field of the mind. There, in that warm, bright place, what the old poet called Mutability does not so quickly come.

But out here on Sunday, October 2, where it rains all day, Dame Mutability never loses. She was in the crowd at Fenway yesterday, a gray day full of bluster and contradiction, when the Red Sox came up in the last of the ninth trailing Baltimore 8–5, while the Yankees, rain-delayed against Detroit, only needing to win one or have Boston lose one to win it all, sat in New York washing down cold cuts with beer and watching the Boston game. Boston had won two, the Yankees had lost two, and suddenly it seemed as if the whole season might go to the last day, or beyond, except here was Boston losing 8–5, while New York sat in its family room and put its feet

up. Lynn, both ankles hurting now as they had in July, hits a single down the right-field line. The crowd stirs. It is on its feet. Hobson, third baseman, former Bear Bryant quarterback, strong, quiet, over 100 RBIs, goes for three breaking balls and is out. The goddess smiles and encourages her agent, a canny journeyman named Nelson Briles.

Now comes a pinch hitter, Bernie Carbo, one-time Rookie of the Year, erratic, quick, a shade too handsome, so laid back he is always, in his soul, stretched out in the tall grass, one arm under his head, watching the clouds and laughing; now he looks over some low stuff unworthy of him and then, uncoiling, sends one out, straight on a right line, over the center-field wall, no cheap Fenway shot, but all of it, the physics as elegant as the arc the ball describes.

New England is on its feet, roaring. The summer will not pass. Roaring, they recall the

THE CYCLE

evening, late and cold, in 1975, the sixth game of the World Series, perhaps the greatest baseball game played in the last fifty years, when Carbo, loose and easy, had uncoiled to tie the game that Fisk would win. It is 8–7, one out, and school will never start, rain will never come, sun will warm the back of your neck forever. Now Bailey, picked up from the National League recently, big arms, heavy gut, experienced, new to the league and the club; he fouls off two and then, checking, tentative, a big man off balance, he pops a soft liner to the first baseman. It is suddenly darker and later, and the announcer doing the game coast to coast, a New Yorker who works for a New York television station, sounds relieved. His little world, well-lit, hot-combed, split-second-timed, had no capacity to absorb this much gritty, grainy, contrary reality.

Cox swings a bat, stretches his long arms, bends his back, the rookie from Pawtucket, who broke in two weeks earlier with a record six straight hits, the kid drafted ahead of Fred Lynn, rangy, smooth, cool. The count runs two-and-two, Briles is cagey, nothing too good, and Cox swings, the ball beginning toward the mound and then, in a jaunty, wayward dance, skipping past Briles, feinting to the right, skimming the last of the grass, finding the dirt, moving now like some small, purposeful marine creature negotiating the green deep, easily avoiding the jagged rock of second base, traveling steady and straight now out into the dark, silent recesses of center field.

The aisles are jammed, the place is on its feet, the wrappers, the programs, the Coke cups and peanut shells, the detritus of an afternoon; the anxieties, the things that have to be done tomorrow, the regrets about yesterday, the accumulation of a summer: all forgotten, while hope, the anchor, bites and takes hold where a moment before it seemed we would be swept out with the tide. Rice is up, Rice whom Aaron had said was the only one he'd seen with the ability to break his records, Rice the best clutch hitter on the club, with the best slugging percentage in the league, Rice, so quick and strong he once

checked his swing halfway through and snapped the bat in two, Rice the Hammer of God sent to scourge the Yankees, the sound was overwhelming, fathers pounded their sons on the back, cars pulled off the road, households froze, New England exulted in its blessedness, and roared its thanks for all good things, for Rice and for a summer stretching halfway through October. Briles threw, Rice swung, and it was over. One pitch, a fly to center, and it stopped. Summer died in New England and like rain sliding off a roof, the crowd slipped out of Fenway, quickly, with only a steady murmur of concern for the drive ahead remaining of the roar. Mutability had turned the seasons and translated hope to memory once again. And once again, she had used baseball, our best invention to stay change, to bring change on. That is why it breaks my heart, that game—not because in New York they could win because Boston lost; in that, there is a rough justice, and a reminder to the Yankees of how slight and fragile are the circumstances that exalt one group of human beings over another. It breaks my heart because it was meant to foster in me again the illusion that there was something abiding, some pattern and some impulse that could come together to make a reality that would resist the corrosion; and because after it had fostered again that most hungered-for illusion, the game was meant to stop, and betray precisely what it promised.

Of course, there are those who learn after the first few times. They grow out of sports. And there are others who were born with the wisdom to know that nothing lasts. These are the truly tough among us, the ones who can live without illusion, or without even the hope of illusion. I am not that grown-up or up-to-date. I am a simpler creature, tied to more primitive patterns and cycles. I need to think something lasts forever, and it might as well be that state of being that is a game; it might as well be that, in a green field, in the sun. ❖

144

Play at First by John Dobbs, 1980–82.

The Baseball Game
by Andrew Radcliffe, 1986.

Baseball

◆

LINDA PASTAN

When you tried to tell me
baseball was a metaphor

for life: the long, dusty travail
around the bases, for instance,

to try to go home again;
the Sacrifice for which you win

approval but not applause;
the way the light closes down

in the last days of the season—
I didn't believe you.

It's just a way of passing
the time, I said.

And you said: that's it.
Yes.

Chapter V

WAIT TILL NEXT YEAR

148

TO BE BORN AND RAISED in Boston or Chicago is a burden many baseball fans bear with courage. "No team is worshiped with such a perverse sense of fatality," author Thomas Boswell says of the Red Sox. Those of us who endured the expansion years of the Blue Jays, even though we were eventually rewarded beyond all expectation, recognize and admire that spirit. After all, we're in the same division as the damn Yankees.

Faith is the "victory that overcometh the world," the New Testament says. It's a familiar sentiment. "For if there be no faith among the children of men," echoes the Book of Mormon, "God can do no miracle among them." Congregations waiting for miracles in Fenway Park, Wrigley Field, and other houses of worship throughout the nation repeat these litanies without end—though usually in syntax closer to the motto of Mets fans: "You gotta believe." (As Dick Schaap quipped in August 1965, during a Mets road trip, "There was one happy note for Mets fans. If the Mets are going to break their all-time losing record of 17 games, established in 1962, they will do it at home, where it will be appreciated.")

To have one's faith tested and found strong is so much a part of baseball's character that there are those who consider it essential. They ask each other: What do Yankee fans know about baseball? Anyone can love a winner. It takes guts to back the Bosox. Waiting is even tougher for the players. Patience and humility are elemental in baseball—as the hero of Eliot Asinof's *Man on Spikes* learns before his first major league game.

Filling that gap between desire and reality is the fantasy of what will be. Robert Coover creates an entire fantasy league in *The Universal Baseball Association, Inc.*; Sherwood Anderson spies a man play-acting at home.

Everyone here holds out hope for one more shot at glory. How fitting that the baseball season begins in the season of renewal.

[OPPOSITE]
Boys' Life cover,
June 1935.

Baseball fantasies

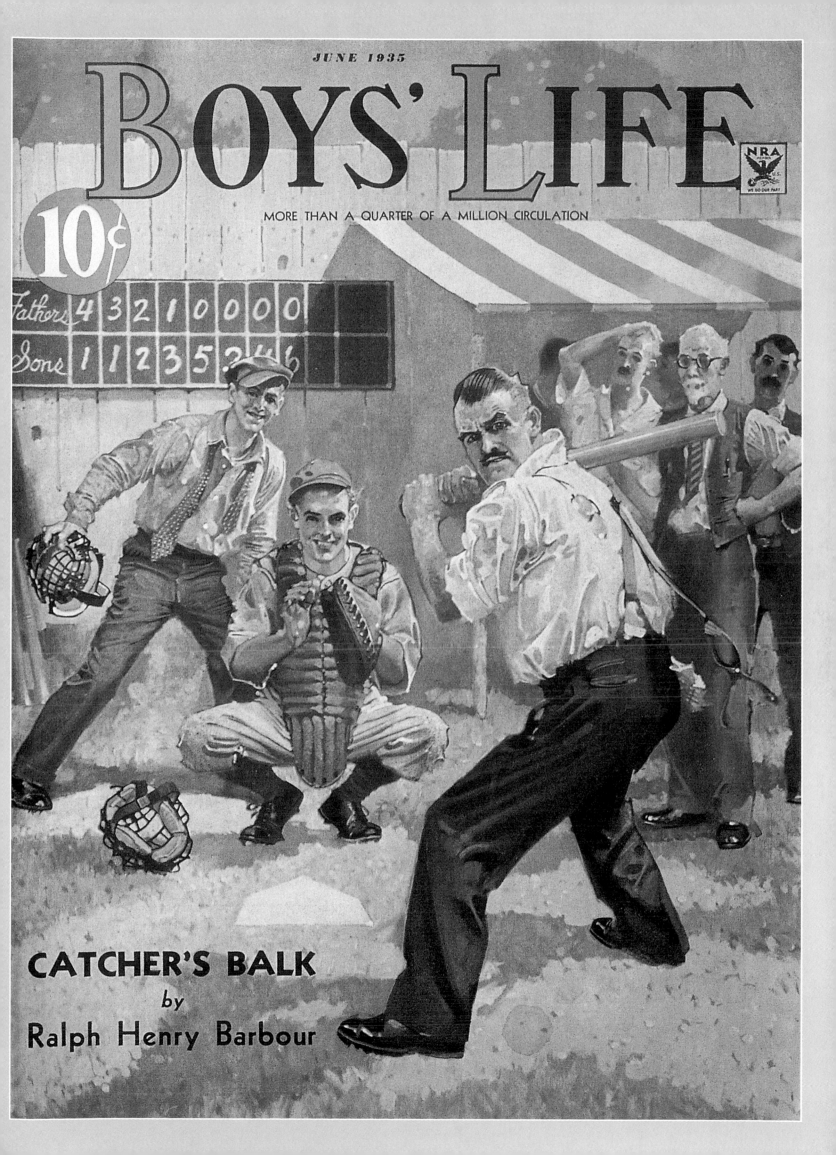

"The Red Sox truly are the boys of summer. It's always been the fall that's given them trouble."

—DAN SHAUGHNESSY

Boston Batter by Gerald Garston, 1990.

Baseball at Night **by Morris Kantor, 1976.**

Dreaming of Baseball

◆

RON McFARLAND

Late summer nights I dream of baseball
coming back to small towns.
                              Bleachers return
filled with genuine splinters,
so I rent a flat canvas cushion and lean back
arching my spine
                    to the next row.

Moths in the lights make better butterflies
than these nine guys
                          make ballplayers.
Behind the stands, preparing for life,
boys shag fouls,
                    trade profanities,
invest themselves in casual fistfights.

Three loud women, always the first ones there,
hold court behind home plate.
                              One of them knows me,
even behind my scorecard. I give her my
smallest wave,
                    my slenderest smile.

Above the dugout adolescent wives of the home team
languish in blonde boredom.
                              Forcing their squeals,
they hope their husbands will grow up some day
and find real jobs,
                        and they can stop
checking groceries, waiting tables.
They all feel pregnant.

I buy a Pepsi from the sad-eyed boy who moves
gloomily through the stands in search of his boyhood.
He drops my change.
                    Hope dwindles.
                              Our team
fades in the steam from the showers
under the left-field bleachers.

The myopic umpire yawns through the sixth inning.
He doesn't care who's pinch-hitting,
                              who's in relief.
But suddenly we do.
                    Suddenly the game is crucial.
Two on, two out. The three fat women, their hearts at bat,

razz the umpire, curse the visiting coach.

Someone in the boxes calls the ump a jerk.
It's the Baptist minister,
                        his best sermon ever.
Applause and laughter.
                        He should run for mayor.
With a crimson nod he returns to his folding chair.
Sudden silence. A bat swishes the air.

Below the stands the ballplayers shrug, their sweat
evaporating.
                    Somebody snaps the catcher's jockstrap.
In the parking lot his blonde wife
lights discreet cigarettes
                        and talks of feeling
tired and pregnant.

The fattest woman says she hates these umpires,
says she'll buy the beer.
                        I dream of nights like this.

[OPPOSITE]
Leonardo Series: NOW/runner 4
by Charles Hobson, 1990.

From
Hello Towns

◆

SHERWOOD ANDERSON

HE DID NOT KNOW I WAS COMING. . . . The man was in his house alone and had become in fancy a ball player. I saw what happened through a window. The man was squatting, with his hands on his knees, in the living room of his house. He had become a shortstop and was all alert. I dare say someone like Babe Ruth was at bat. When the man had gone to the cities to see the professionals play he had noted how the infielders kept talking to each other.

"Now, Ed. Careful now, Ed. Watch him, Ed!" I heard the photographer cry. He spoke sharply to the pitcher. "Get it over the plate, Bill!" he cried.

It was evident the batter had made a hit. I saw him dash across the room for second base. He had knocked over a chair on the way, but he did not care. He had made the play.

I saw him receive the ball and throw to first. There was an intent look in his eyes. Would the ball get to first ahead of the runner? It did. "Ah," I heard him sigh with relief.

It goes without saying that I went away and returned on the next day. . . . ❖

155

Infield: Jelks by **John Hull, 1989.**

A Dream of Third Base

for Sterling Watson

◆

PETER MEINKE

Night after night, frozen at third base,
I lean toward a throw I know I must catch
but don't stretch far enough:
the ball sails off, the runner
slides snarling at my feet. Then
right away and once again—
bare-handed as before the fall—
perched on third in the starless air,
the runner's shadow darkening the path,
I wait for that accursed ball.

I think I'm afraid it will hurt:
the ball is coming too fast;
the catcher with his thick wrists
has reared and fired like a loaded gun—
or the snake-armed shortstop whose lidless eyes . . .

Surely baseball stands for something else—
I haven't been a fan
since the Dodgers abandoned Ebbet's Field;
we used to go on Sunday, my dad and I,
breaking the Fourth Commandment . . .

The field is Paradise, then, all green and new:
we're young and quick of foot, our cries
rise in the springtime air.

And then we're given a ball.
And then we're given a bat.
Who are those men in black?

It starts hurting after that.

But why, for me, that place? "Nel mezzo
del cammin di nostra vita, I awoke on third base."

Dante would have loved baseball, all those nines
and threes (even the stands stand
for something else: howling gluttons
stuff hot dogs down their throats).
I crouch at third, the corner eternally hot,
with Eros on the mound and Thanatos at bat—
while the citizens stomp their feet,
waving doleful undershirts—
remembering the thick wrists of my father,
the infield's skin, the ball with its stitches turning;
drafted into this dream
by some archetypal team
my cleats dig into the dirt,
my hand already burning:
guilty, small, and hurt.

157

[FOLLOWING PAGES]
Out at Third
by Nelson Rosenberg, undated.
The Phillips Collection,
Washington, D.C.

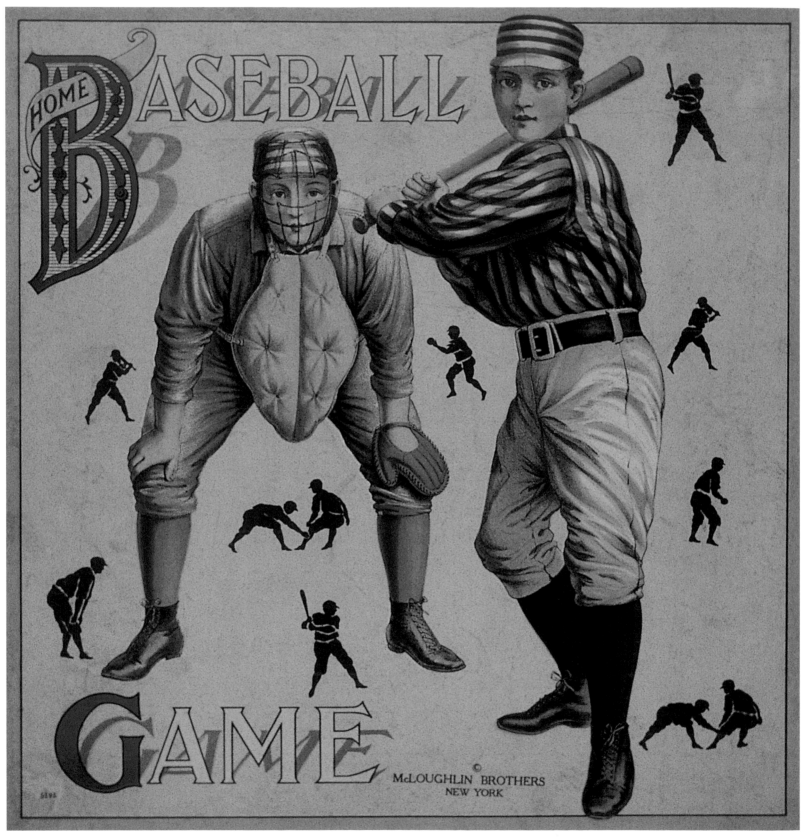

McLoughlin Baseball Game, ca. 1888.

From

The Universal Baseball Association, Inc.; J. Henry Waugh, Prop.

◆

ROBERT COOVER

WHEN HE'D FINALLY DECIDED to settle on his own baseball game, Henry had spent the better part of two months just working with the problem of odds and equilibrium points in an effort to approximate that complexity. Two dice had not done it. He'd tried three, each a different color, and the 216 different combinations had provided the complexity, all right, but he'd nearly gone blind trying to sort the colors on each throw. Finally, he'd compromised, keeping the three dice, but all white, reducing the total number of combinations to 56, though of course the odds were still based on 216. To restore—and, in fact, to intensify—the complexity of the multicolored method, he'd allowed triple ones and sixes—1-1-1 and 6-6-6—to trigger the more spectacular events, by referring the following dice throw to what he called his Stress Chart, also a three-dice chart but far more dramatic in nature than the basic ones. Two successive throws of triple ones and sixes were exceedingly rare— only about three times in every two entire seasons of play on the average—but when it happened, the next throw was referred, finally, to the Chart of Extraordinary Occurrences, where just about anything from fistfights to fixed ball games could happen. These two charts were what gave the game its special quality, making it much more than just a series of hits and walks and outs. Besides these, he also had special strategy charts for hit-and-run plays, attempted stolen bases, sacrifice bunts, and squeeze plays, still others for deciding the ages of rookies when they came up, for providing details of injuries and errors, and for determining who, each year, must die. ❖

The Saturday Evening Post cover by John Falter, September 2, 1950.

From

Diamonds Are Forever

◆

WILFRID SHEED

FOR ANYONE WHO BELIEVES that baseball was born in a big-league stadium, the small-town casualness (at least in the towns I've seen) brings balm to the spirit. You are tethered to no particular seat. The usher, if you can find her, doubles as business manager and anything else that needs doing, though she always has time for a chat.

On beer nights, you wander with the gang to that end of the field. Otherwise you watch a bit behind third and a bit behind first, until you have a panascope of the game that television is still striving for. The mood is strictly county fair, with the loudspeaker reeling off an endless list of raffles and lucky winners. The inevitable female camp-followers, or "baseball Annies," are on hand to check the talent, but they are

startlingly young and fresh-looking, and when they make off later with their pink-faced prizes, with a merry squeal of tires, you feel sure they're heading for ice cream and nothing but ice cream.

However, if not, not. You've had a mellow evening yourself, and let the world do what it likes. This could be the real Middle America at that, as far from book-banning as it is from downtown vandalism. After a last bite of cordon bleu hot dog (why do they taste so great outdoors?), you race the flickering stadium lights (which were never that strong to begin with) to the parking lot—where, so help me, you find one of the young athletes still playing pepper with some small fry. . . .

There is a diamond chain running from

PONY League through Little League to Babe Ruth (which gets you through age 15), and after that, American Legion to 18 or semi-pro where available, and at last some colleges that teach baseball as seriously as they teach football; then on to various degrees of minors and finally the brass ring itself, toward which the whole chain strains; and blessed are those who follow it all the way. Or even part of the way. A guy who's played one game in the pros is like a former State Senator, a big man in most neighborhoods, and any saloon, as long as he lives.

But suppose you just go bumping along the bottom all your life, playing pick-up softball with fellow physical defectives? Well, life can be sweet at the bottom, too, and there's always plenty of room there, with leagues beneath leagues, for infants, old folk and just plain incompetents. And if you can't stand all that organization, you can simply organize a disorganized game, as we have in my neighborhood. Wherever you wind up, you will find yourself with better equipment and less menacing surfaces than we had as kids.

The only thing we did prove for good in those deprived, pre-Korean glove days was that Americans will stop at nothing to play with a bat and a ball: stickball, stoopball, wallball—every alley and cow pasture dictated how you played there, just as imperiously as Fenway Park. For bats, everything from broom handles to rolled magazines (excellent for libraries) was pressed into service; as for balls, the great Paul Waner learned to bat by striking corn cobs, whereas the current National League batting champion, Tony Gwynn, worked out against a soxball, i.e., a sock rolled tight inside a rubber band. In the wartime '40s it was a melancholy rite of spring to watch the season's ball start to unravel. You could shore it up for a while with tape, but the tape weighed like lead and could easily break the season's bat. We played on grimly with the remains.

The true zealot wants his baseball with him everywhere he goes, even to bed, where he can play it electronically on the ceiling, or by inventing his own private league (as in Robert Coover's classic book, *The Universal Baseball Association, Inc.; J. Henry Waugh, Prop.*) or by phoning a fellow addict for relief. But for the average citizen, simply trotting out onto the spring grass, and maybe backhanding a grounder and flipping it, and bathing one's ears once more in the immemorial chatter—"Only takes one to hit one," "'S'lookin' 'em over," "No pitcher, no pitcher"—will do.

To such a fan, an American summer without those sounds would be as empty as Rachel Carson's *Silent Spring*. Those piping chirps of "A walk's as good as a hit" are like crickets in August. Where do they go in the winter, anyway? Some fly South, others disappear into the closet, where, I suspect, fans mouth them silently as they pound their mitts.

But right now the voice of the umpire is heard once again in the land, the ducks are on the pond and the goose hangs high. The season isn't over till it's over, but the cliches can already beat you a lot of ways. If the mark of a grand passion is that you can love it even when it's kind of dumb, then baseball wins out by inches, one game at a time. Baseball is pre-eminently the talking man's game and who cares, or even notices, if the conversation is sometimes awesomely dull?

The big-league mystique totters on, because it is existentially necessary, as we used to say at Ebbets Field. Without it, the whole diamond chain breaks. The big time is the vision of heaven that keeps the peasants toiling cheerfully in Waterloo, Iowa, and in your own backyard. And even the nonbeliever bends his knee to the World Series.

But if the simple pleasures of loyalty and team spirit are not to be found at the top—except among winners and on a one-year lease—they must be sought a little lower down. The biggies will always be loved and returned to for their icy perfection. But for everyday comfort and satisfaction, there's a lot to be said for the game next door. ❖

163

From
Man on Spikes

◆

ELIOT ASINOF

IT WAS WEIRD, THE WAY IT HAPPENED. He was just about to go for a walk with Laura, a simple little morning walk that would take them away for a lingering breakfast in a pleasant family restaurant they enjoyed. He was sitting on the bed, watching her finish dressing. She was putting on a fall suit for the first time, and it crossed his mind that she was doing it to remind him that the summer was ending, and another winter coming on. The thought set off a depressing chain of emotions. It was then that the phone rang and he listened to the peremptory orders from Chicago. They came so suddenly that he became dizzy. Afterwards he had to lie back on the bed to ease the shock.

He had to hurry with Laura to catch the plane. Now he thought sourly, Two minutes later and I wouldn't have been there to receive the call.

They flew down to Chicago a few hours before game time and taxied directly to the ball park, with hardly time to catch a bite to eat. Sixteen years he had plugged away for this chance. When they finally found they needed him, they threw it in his face like an insult.

In the locker room before the game, he knew the others were watching him dress, but he didn't care. A thirty-five-year-old rookie was something of a freak. Those who knew him saw his determination and understood. To the others it was simply a matter of winning a pennant and the pile of dough that goes with it. But to Mike it was more, much more. He looked at them quickly, responding to their greetings. He knew that some must be thinking he was good, as good as almost any of them, and if the ball had bounced differently, it might have been Kutner up there all these years instead of them. But now he was thirty-five, and he could be called old. He saw those who did not know him look curiously across the room at the partially bald head, the dark leathery skin of his neck, the heavy, uneven walk; and he thought they'd be wondering how many years they had left for themselves. Respectfully, they had left him alone while he dressed.

Mike had waited to finish until they were all out. His uniform was clean and he liked its fresh, sterile smell. He laced his shoes tightly and put on his new cap. With pride he didn't bother to conceal, he walked over to the big mirror by the shower room and stood solidly before it. He looked at himself for a long moment, allowing the glow to penetrate. The excitement of it tickled the back of his neck, bringing goose pimples to his skin. He had never felt so wonderful.

"You're here, Mike . . . ," he said out loud. "You finally made it! "Then he clenched his fists as the emotion welled up within him. "You're here, goddammit, and you're not going back!"

Behind him, he heard the scuffle of heels on the concrete floor. He shifted his focus briefly to see an old man coming down the aisle. Finally, he turned from the mirror to get his glove, suddenly conscious that the man had stopped and was watching him for a longer time than Mike felt natural. But this was not the time to wonder and he closed his locker and got ready to leave for the diamond.

Then he heard him, and at once it began to make sense.

"Hello, Kutner."

Mike spun around to face him, drawn by a quality in the voice he somehow recognized. He saw the old man, older-looking than anyone he thought he knew, wrinkled and squint-eyed, yet erect and alert. He saw the smile as he moved toward the outstretched hand, and at once his memory bridged the gap.

"Hello, Mr. Fain," he said.

They shook hands warmly, and Mike met his piercing eyes.

"I was in Chicago for this Philly series, Kutner. I heard you were here. Just thought I'd drop back to say hello."

The words sounded trivial as he said them, too trivial for the importance of the moment. But their hands remained clasped for a long moment, covering the silence between them, and he saw in Durkin Fain's searching look that he felt deeply about Mike Kutner's finally making it.

What do you see, old man? Don't compare me with the kid you went out on a limb for. You're looking at an aging athlete, tired, almost bald, as old in his profession as you are in yours. Remember what you said, Mr. Fain: "I'm gonna make you a major leaguer." That's what you told me.

Sure. Here I am.

But this ain't what you meant, Mr. Fain. This ain't the way you meant it to be. I shouldn't be a rookie, Mr. Fain. I sure as hell don't look like one.

He looked hard at the old scout again, suddenly tired of this feeble self-examination. He could see the other man now and the brutal thing that the years had done to him.

"I heard you've been coaching the college boys, Mr. Fain."

The old man smiled. "No more, son. Too old to do that well. I haven't been up to it the last year or two."

Mike didn't know what to say to him. He turned back to his locker and grabbed the fifty-cent cigar he'd bought at the terminal. He had planned to smoke it later, as a kind of celebration for himself.

"Here, Mr. Fain," he said. "Have a cigar for old time's sake."

Fain took it, and put it in his pocket.

"Thanks," he said briefly.

"Don't you smoke 'em any more?"

Durkin Fain nodded.

"This one . . . after the game."

Mike nodded. He tightened his belt and started to the door, stopped and looked back. It was all so brief, so incomplete. There was nothing said. After all these years, there was nothing to say. It seemed strange, for he had thought of the scout a thousand times.

Fain smiled at him.

"Have a good day, son," he said, and then he nodded. "It ain't never too late." ❖

Man on First by James Chapin, 1948.

From
Wait Till Next Year
◆

DORIS KEARNS GOODWIN

WHEN I WAS SIX, my father gave me a bright-red scorebook that opened my heart to the game of baseball. After dinner on long summer nights, he would sit beside me in our small enclosed porch to hear my account of that day's Brooklyn Dodger game. Night after night he taught me the odd collection of symbols, numbers, and letters that enable a baseball lover to record every action of the game. Our score sheets had blank boxes in which we could draw our own slanted lines in the form of a diamond as we followed players around the bases. Wherever the baserunner's progress stopped, the line stopped. He instructed me to fill in the unused boxes at the end of each inning with an elaborate checkerboard design which made it absolutely clear who had been the last to bat and who would lead off the next inning. By the time I had mastered the art of scorekeeping, a lasting bond had been forged among my father, baseball, and me.

All through the summer of 1949, my first summer as a fan, I spent my afternoons sitting cross-legged before the squat Philco radio which stood as a permanent fixture on our porch in Rockville Centre, on the South Shore of Long Island, New York. With my scorebook spread before me, I attended Dodger games through the courtly voice of Dodger announcer Red Barber. As he announced the lineup, I carefully printed each player's name in a column on the left side of my sheet. Then, using the standard system my father had taught me, which assigned a number to each position in the field, starting with a "1" for the pitcher and ending with a "9" for the right fielder, I recorded every play. I found it difficult at times to sit still. As the Dodgers came to bat, I would walk around the room, talking to the players as if they were standing in front of me. At critical junctures, I tried to make a bargain, whispering and cajoling while Pee Wee Reese or Duke Snider stepped

Night Ball Game
by Ferdinand E. Warren, 1946.
Georgia Museum of Art.

into the batter's box: "Please, please, get a hit. If you get a hit now, I'll make my bed every day for a week." Sometimes, when the score was close and the opposing team at bat with men on base, I was too agitated to listen. Asking my mother to keep notes, I left the house for a walk around the block, hoping that when I returned the enemy threat would be over, and once again we'd be up

Jackie Robinson
by Lance Richbourg, 1988.

at bat. Mostly, however, I stayed at my post, diligently recording each inning so that, when my father returned from his job as bank examiner for the State of New York, I could re-create for him the game he had missed.

When my father came home from the city, he would change from his three-piece suit into long pants and a short-sleeved sport shirt, and come downstairs for the ritual Manhattan cocktail with my mother. Then my parents would summon me for dinner from my play on the street outside our house. All through dinner I had to restrain myself from telling him about the day's game, waiting for the special time to come when we would sit together on the couch, my scorebook on my lap.

"Well, did anything interesting happen today?" he would begin. And even before the daily question was completed I had eagerly launched into my narrative of every play, and almost every pitch, of that afternoon's contest. It never crossed my mind to wonder if, at the close of a day's work, he might find my lengthy account the least bit tedious. For there was mastery as well as pleasure in our nightly ritual. Through my knowledge, I commanded my father's undivided attention, the sign of his love. It would instill in me an early awareness of the power of narrative, which would introduce a lifetime of storytelling, fueled by the naive confidence that others would find me as entertaining as my father did.

Michael Francis Aloysius Kearns, my father, was a short man who appeared much larger on account of his erect bearing, broad chest, and thick neck. He had a ruddy Irish complexion, and his green eyes flashed with humor and vitality. When he smiled his entire face was transformed, radiating enthusiasm and friendliness. He called me "Bubbles," a pet name he had chosen, he told me, because I seemed to enjoy so many things. Anxious to confirm his description, I refused to let my enthusiasm wane, even when I grew tired or grumpy. Thus excitement about things became a habit, a part of my personality, and the expectation that I should enjoy new experiences often engendered the enjoyment itself.

These nightly recountings of the Dodgers' progress provided my first lessons in the narrative art. From the scorebook, with its tight squares of neatly arranged symbols, I could unfold the tale of an entire game and tell a story that seemed to last almost as long as the game itself. At first, I was unable to resist the temptation to skip ahead to an important play in later innings. At times, I grew so excited about a Dodger victory that I blurted out the final score before I had hardly begun. But as I became more

experienced in my storytelling, I learned to build a dramatic story with a beginning, middle, and end. Slowly, I learned that if I could recount the game, one batter at a time, inning by inning, without divulging the outcome, I could keep the suspense and my father's interest alive until the very last pitch. Sometimes I pretended that I was the great Red Barber himself, allowing my voice to swell when reporting a home run, quieting to a whisper when the action grew tense, injecting tidbits about the players into my reports. At critical moments, I would jump from the couch to illustrate a ball that turned foul at the last moment or a dropped fly that was scored as an error.

"How many hits did Roy Campanella get?" my dad would ask. Tracing my finger across the horizontal line that represented Campanella's at bats that day, I would count. "One, two, three. Three hits, a single, a double, and another single." "How many strikeouts for Don Newcombe?" It was easy. I would count the Ks. "One, two . . . eight. He had eight strikeouts." Then he'd ask me more subtle questions about different plays—whether a strikeout was called or swinging, whether the double play was around the horn, whether the single that won the game was hit to left or right. If I had scored carefully, using the elaborate system he had taught me, I would know the answers. My father pointed to the second inning, where Jackie Robinson had hit a single and then stolen second. There was excitement in his voice. "See, it's all here. While Robinson was dancing off second, he rattled the pitcher so badly that the next two guys walked to load the bases. That's the impact Robinson makes, game after game. Isn't he something?" His smile at such moments inspired me to take my responsibility seriously.

Sometimes, a particular play would trigger in my father a memory of a similar situation in a game when he was young, and he would tell me stories about the Dodgers when he was a boy growing up in Brooklyn. His vivid tales featured strange heroes such as Casey Stengel, Zack

Catcher on the Line
by Robert Riggs, undated.

Wheat, and Jimmy Johnston. Though it was hard
at first to imagine that the Casey Stengel I knew,
the manager of the Yankees, with his colorful
language and hilarious antics, was the same man
as the Dodger outfielder who hit an inside-the-
park home run at the first game ever played at

bases loaded, and through a series of mishaps on the base paths, three Dodgers ended up at third base at the same time. And I was sitting by my father's side, five years before I was born, when the lights were turned on for the first time at Ebbets Field, the crowd gasping and then cheering as the summer night was transformed into startling day.

When I had finished describing the game, it was time to go to bed, unless I could convince my father to tally each player's batting average, reconfiguring his statistics to reflect the developments of that day's game. If Reese went 3 for 5 and had started the day at .303, my father showed me, by adding and multiplying all the numbers in his head, that his average would rise to .305. If Snider went 0 for 4 and started the day at .301, then his average would dip four points below the .300 mark. If Carl Erskine had let in three runs in seven innings, then my father would multiply three times nine, divide that by the number of innings pitched, and magically tell me whether Erskine's earned-run average had improved or worsened. It was this facility with numbers that had made it possible for my father to pass the civil-service test and become a bank examiner despite leaving school after the eighth grade. And this job had carried him from a Brooklyn tenement to a house with a lawn on Southard Avenue in Rockville Centre.

All through that summer, my father kept from me the knowledge that running box scores appeared in the daily newspapers. He never mentioned that these abbreviated histories had been a staple feature of the sports pages since the nineteenth century and were generally the first thing he and his fellow commuters turned to when they opened the *Daily News* and the *Herald Tribune* in the morning. I believed that, if I did not recount the games he had missed, my father would never have been able to follow our Dodgers the proper way, day by day, play by play, inning by inning. In other words, without me, his love of baseball would be forever unfulfilled. ❖

173

Ebbets Field, my father so skillfully stitched together the past and the present that I felt as if I were living in different time zones. If I closed my eyes, I imagined I was at Ebbets Field in the 1920s for that celebrated game when Dodger right fielder Babe Herman hit a double with the

Untitled
by Jeffrey Rubin, 2000.

From
The Interior Stadium

◆

ROGER ANGELL

WITHIN THE BALLPARK, time moves differently, marked by no clock except the events of the game. This is the unique, unchangeable feature of baseball and perhaps explains why this sport, for all the enormous changes it has undergone in the past decade or two, remains somehow rustic, unviolent, and introspective. Baseball's time is seamless and invisible, a bubble within which players move at exactly the same pace and rhythms as all their predecessors. This is the way the game was played in our youth and in our fathers' youth, and even back then—back in the country days—there must have been the same feeling that time could be stopped. Since baseball time is measured only in outs, all you have to do is succeed utterly; keep hitting, keep the rally alive, and you have defeated time. You remain forever young. Sitting in the stands, we sense this, if only dimly. The players below us—Mays, DiMaggio, Ruth, Snodgrass—swim and blur in memory, the ball floats over to Terry Turner, and the end of this game may never come. ❖

175

Chapter VI

KNUCKLE BALLS

A BAND IN THE BLEACHERS PLAYS "Three Blind Mice" when the umpire makes a lousy call. A heckler yells to a struggling batter, "Flip over the plate and read the directions!" Baseball may be serious stuff, especially as October approaches, but it can be hard to keep a straight face. Even with the season on the line, no one complains about a carnival atmosphere at the stadium.

Baseball has a long tradition of clowning. "Who's on First" was a vaudeville routine long before Bud Abbott and Lou Costello adopted and perfected it. And though some people refuse to take baseball seriously, others are too solemn. Fortunately, their grim reverence is no match for the likes of Frank Sullivan's "The Cliché Expert Testifies on Baseball."

Then there's the humor from the players themselves. Reporter Jonathan Yardley once noted, "Ballplayers may be only occasionally noted for depth of intellect, but when it comes to wit they're often as deft, quick, and agile as they are with bat and glove; at times a baseball locker room resembles a graduate-level seminar in badinage and repartee." Even if Yogi Berra didn't say everything he said, ballplayers' humor, when printable, has a gentle sarcasm that follows naturally from being asked convoluted questions about why they whiffed. Some questions just don't deserve a straight answer.

The lighter side of the game

"There is one word in America that says it all, and that one word is 'You never know.'"

—JOAQUIN ANDUJAR

[OPPOSITE]
The First Pitch
by Arnold Roth, 2000.

Who's on First

◆

BUD ABBOTT AND LOU COSTELLO

ABBOTT: You know, strange as it may seem, they give ball players nowadays very peculiar names. . . . Now, on the Cooperstown team we have Who's on first, What's on second, I Don't Know is on third—

COSTELLO: That's what I want to find out. I want you to tell me the names of the fellows on the Cooperstown team.

ABBOTT: I'm telling you. Who's on first, What's on second, I Don't Know is on third.

COSTELLO: You know the fellow's names?

ABBOTT: Yes.

COSTELLO: Well, then, who's playin' first?

ABBOTT: Yes.

COSTELLO: I mean the fellow's name on first base.

ABBOTT: Who.

COSTELLO: The fellow's name on first base for Cooperstown.

ABBOTT: Who.

COSTELLO: The guy on first base.

ABBOTT: Who is on first base.

COSTELLO: Well, what are you asking me for?

ABBOTT: I'm not asking you—I am telling you. Who is on first.

COSTELLO: I'm asking you—who's on first?

ABBOTT: That's the man's name.

COSTELLO: That's who's name?

ABBOTT: Yes.

COSTELLO: Well, go ahead, tell me!

ABBOTT: Who.

COSTELLO: The guy on first.

ABBOTT: Who.

COSTELLO: The first baseman.

ABBOTT: Who is on first.

COSTELLO: Have you got a first baseman on first?

ABBOTT: Certainly.

COSTELLO: Well, all I'm trying to find out is what's the guy's name on first base.

ABBOTT: Oh, no, no, What is on second base.

COSTELLO: I'm not asking you who's on second.

ABBOTT: Who's on first.

COSTELLO: That's what I'm trying to find out.

ABBOTT: Well, don't change the players around.

COSTELLO: I'm not changing anybody.

ABBOTT: Now, take it easy.

COSTELLO: What's the guy's name on first base?

ABBOTT: What's the guy's name on second base.

COSTELLO: I'm not askin' ya who's on second.

ABBOTT: Who's on first.

COSTELLO: I don't know.

ABBOTT: He's on third. We're not talking about him.

COSTELLO: How could I get on third base?

ABBOTT: You mentioned his name.

COSTELLO: If I mentioned the third baseman's name, who did I say is playing third?

ABBOTT: No, Who's playing first.

COSTELLO: Stay offa first, will ya?

ABBOTT: Please. Now what is it you want you know?

COSTELLO: What is the fellow's name on third base?

ABBOTT: What is the fellow's name on second base.

COSTELLO: I'm not askin' ya who's on second.

ABBOTT: Who's on first.

COSTELLO: I don't know.

ABBOTT & COSTELLO: Third base.

◆　◆　◆

COSTELLO: (Makes noises.) You got an outfield?

ABBOTT: Oh, sure.

COSTELLO: Cooperstown has got a good outfield?

ABBOTT: Oh, absolutely.

COSTELLO: The left fielder's name?

ABBOTT: Why.

COSTELLO: I don't know, I just thought I'd ask.

ABBOTT: Well, I just thought I'd tell you.

COSTELLO: Then tell me who's playing left field.

ABBOTT: Who's playing first.

COSTELLO: Stay out of the infield.

ABBOTT: Don't mention any names out here.

COSTELLO: I want to know what's the fellow's name in the left field.

ABBOTT: What is on second.

COSTELLO: I'm not asking you who's on second.

ABBOTT: Who is on first.

COSTELLO: I don't know.

ABBOTT & COSTELLO: Third base.

COSTELLO: (Makes noises.)

ABBOTT: Now take it easy, man.

COSTELLO: And the left fielder's name?

ABBOTT: Why.

COSTELLO: Because.

ABBOTT: Oh, he's center field.

COSTELLO: Wait a minute. You got a pitcher on the team?

ABBOTT: Wouldn't this be a fine team without a pitcher.

COSTELLO: I don't know. Tell me the pitcher's name.

ABBOTT: Tomorrow.

COSTELLO: You don't want to tell me today?

ABBOTT: I'm telling you, man.

COSTELLO: Then go ahead.

ABBOTT: Tomorrow.

COSTELLO: What time?

ABBOTT: What time what?

COSTELLO: What time tomorrow are you gonna tell me who's pitching?

ABBOTT: Now listen, Who is not pitching. Who is on—.

COSTELLO: I'll break your arm if you say who's on first.

ABBOTT: Then why come up here and ask?

COSTELLO: I want to know what's the pitcher's name.

ABBOTT: What's on second.

COSTELLO: I don't know.

ABBOTT & COSTELLO: Third base.

◆　◆　◆

COSTELLO: Ya gotta catcher?

ABBOTT: Yes.

COSTELLO: The catcher's name.

ABBOTT: Today.

COSTELLO: Today. And Tomorrow's pitching.

ABBOTT: Now you've got it.

COSTELLO: That's all. Cooperstown got a couple of days on their team. That's all.

ABBOTT: Well, I can't help that.

COSTELLO: (Makes noises.)

ABBOTT: Alright. What do you want me to do?

COSTELLO: Gotta catcher?

ABBOTT: Yes.

COSTELLO: I'm a good catcher too, you know.

ABBOTT: I know that.

COSTELLO: I would like to play for the Coooperstown team.

ABBOTT: Well, I might arrange that.

COSTELLO: I would like to catch. Now I'm being a good catcher, Tomorrow's pitching on the team and I'm catching.

ABBOTT: Yes.

COSTELLO: Tomorrow throws the ball and the guy up bunts the ball.

ABBOTT: Yes.

COSTELLO: Now when he bunts the ball—me being a good catcher—I want to throw the guy

182

Cast iron painted andirons, late nineteenth–early twentieth century.

out at first base, so I pick up the ball and throw it to who?

ABBOTT: Now, that's the first thing you said right.

COSTELLO: I DON'T EVEN KNOW WHAT I'M TALKING ABOUT.

ABBOTT: Well, that's all you have to do.

COSTELLO: Is throw to first base.

ABBOTT: Yes.

COSTELLO: Now who's got it?

ABBOTT: Naturally.

COSTELLO: Who has it?

ABBOTT: Naturally.

COSTELLO: Naturally.

ABBOTT: Naturally.

COSTELLO: I throw the ball to Naturally.

ABBOTT: You throw the ball to Who.

COSTELLO: Naturally.

ABBOTT: Naturally. Well, say it that way.

COSTELLO: That's what I'm saying.

ABBOTT: Now don't get excited. Now don't get excited.

COSTELLO: I throw the ball to first base.

ABBOTT: Then Who gets it.

COSTELLO: He better get it.

ABBOTT: That's it. All right now, don't get excited. Take it easy.

COSTELLO: Hmmmmmph.

ABBOTT: Hmmmmmph.

COSTELLO: Now I throw the ball to first base, whoever it is grabs the ball, so the guy runs to second.

ABBOTT: Uh-huh.

COSTELLO: Who picks up the ball and throws it to What. What throws it to I Don't Know. I Don't Know throws it back to Tomorrow—a triple play.

ABBOTT: Yeah. It could be.

COSTELLO: Another guy gets up and it's a long fly ball to center. Why? I don't know. And I don't care.

ABBOTT: What was that?

COSTELLO: I said, I don't care.

ABBOTT: Oh, that's our shortstop. ❖

[FOLLOWING PAGES]
Unfolded score card cover, ca. 1885.

SHORT STOP.

HOT LINER AT SHORT.

1ST BASEMAN.

GUARDING FIRST BASE.

Yogi Berra by Earl Mayan for *The Saturday Evening Post* cover, March 20, 1957.

"I Really Didn't Say Everything I Said"

◆

YOGI BERRA

"It ain't over 'til it's over."
[*During the 1973 National League pennant race*]

"Baseball is ninety percent mental, the other half is physical."

"You give a hundred percent in the first half of the game, and if that isn't enough, in the second half you give what's left."

"Slump? I ain't in no slump. I just ain't hittin'."

"Most of his home runs were hit on artificial turf."
[*On being asked why Johnny Bench hit more home runs than he did*]

"This is like déja vù all over again."

"You can observe a lot just by watchin'."

"If you can't imitate him, don't copy him."

"If people don't want to come out to the park, nobody's going to stop them."

MRS. LINDSAY (wife of New York City mayor John Lindsay):
You certainly look cool.
YOGI BERRA: Thanks, you don't look so hot yourself.

"Nobody goes there anymore; it's too crowded."

"When you come to a fork in the road, take it!"

Chicago Cubs scorecard, ca. 1968.

From

The Cliché Expert
Testifies on Baseball

◆

FRANK SULLIVAN

Q: You are an expert in the clichés of baseball—right?

A: I pride myself on being well versed in the stereotypes of our national pastime.

Q: Well, we'll test you. Who plays baseball?

A: Big-league baseball is customarily played by brilliant outfielders, veteran hurlers, powerful sluggers, knuckle-ball artists, towering first basemen, key moundsmen, fleet base runners, ace southpaws, scrappy little shortstops, sensational war vets, ex-college stars, relief artists, rifle-armed twirlers, dependable mainstays, doughty right-handers, streamlined backstops, power-hitting batsmen, redoubtable infielders, erstwhile Dodgers, veteran sparkplugs, sterling moundsmen, aging twirlers, and rookie sensations.

Q: What other names are rookie sensations known by?

A: They are also known as aspiring rookies, sensational newcomers, promising freshmen, ex-sandlotters, highly touted striplings, and youngsters who will bear watching.

Q: What's the manager of a baseball team called?

A: A veteran pilot. Or youthful pilot. But he doesn't manage the team.

Q: No? What does he do?

A: He guides its destinies.

Q: How?

A: By the use of managerial strategy.

Q: Mr. Arbuthnot, please describe the average major-league-baseball athlete.

A: Well, he comes in three sizes, or types. The first type is tall, slim, lean, towering, rangy, huge, husky, big, strapping, sturdy, handsome, powerful, lanky, rawboned, and rugged.

Q: Quite a hunk of athlete.

A: Well, those are the adjectives usage requires for the description of the Type One, or Ted Williams, ballplayer.

Q: What is Type Two like?

A: He is chunky or stocky—that is to say, Yogi Berra.

Q: And the Third?

A: The third type is elongated and does not walk. He is Ol' Satchmo, or Satchel Paige.

Q: What do you mean Satchmo doesn't walk?

A: Not in the sports pages, he doesn't. He ambles.

Q: You mentioned a hurler, Mr. Arbuthnot. What is a hurler?

A: A hurler is a twirler.

Q: Well, what is a twirler?

A: A twirler is a flinger, a tosser. He's a moundsman.

Q: Moundsman?

A: Yes. He officiates on the mound. When the veteran pilot tells a hurler he is to twirl on a given day, that is a mound assignment, and the hurler who has been told to twirl is the mound nominee for that game.

Q: You mean he pitches?

A: That is right. You have cut the Gordian knot. . . .

Q: Mr. Arbuthnot, how do you, as a cliché expert, refer to first base?

A: First base is the initial sack

Q: And second base?

A: The keystone sack.

Q: What's third base called?

A: The hot corner. The first inning is the initial frame, and an inning without runs is a scoreless stanza.

Q: What is one run known as?

A: A lone run, but four runs are known as a quartet of tallies.

Q: What is a baseball?

A: The pill, the horsehide, the old apple, or the sphere.

Q: And what's a bat?

A: The bat is the willow, or the wagon tongue, or the piece of lumber. In the hands of a mighty batsman, it is the mighty bludgeon.

Q: What does a mighty batsman do?

A: He amasses runs. He connects with the old apple. He raps 'em out and he pounds 'em out. He belts 'em and he clouts 'em. . . .

Q: Now, then, Mr. Arbuthnot, the climax of the baseball season is the World Series, is it not?

A: That's right.

Q: And what is the World Series called?

A: It's the fall classic, or crucial contest, also known as the fray, the epic struggle, and the Homeric struggle. It is part of the American scene, like ham and eggs or pumpkin pie. It is a colorful event.

Q: What is it packed with?

A: Thrills. Drama.

Q: What kind of drama?

A: Sheer or tense.

Q: Why does it have to be packed with thrills and drama?

A: Because if it isn't, it becomes drab fray. ❖

Chicago Cubs scorecard, ca. 1969.

American Beauty #4
by Vincent Scilla, 1992.

Fan Valentines

◆

LILLIAN MORRISON

Yours till the pinch hits
Yours till the 7th inning stretches
Yours till pennant races
Yours till pop flies
Yours till the home runs
Yours till the line drives
Yours till the double plays
Yours till batters box

Illustration by Dan Sayre Groesbeck
for *Casey at the Bat*, **1912.**

Casey at the Bat

◆

ERNEST L. THAYER

The outlook wasn't brilliant for the Mudville nine that day;
The score stood four to two with but one inning more to play;
And then, when Cooney died at first, and Barrows did the same,
A sickly silence fell upon the patrons of the game.

A struggling few got up to go, in deep despair. The rest
Clung to that hope which "springs eternal in the human breast";
They thought, If only Casey could but get a whack at that,
We'd put up even money now, with Casey at the bat.

But Flynn preceded Casey, as did also Jimmy Blake,
And the former was a lulu and the latter was a cake;
So, upon that stricken multitude grim melancholy sat,
For there seemed but little chance of Casey's getting to the bat.

But Flynn let drive a single, to the wonderment of all,
And Blake, the much despised, tore the cover off the ball,
And when the dust had lifted and men saw what had occurred,
There was Jimmy safe at second, and Flynn a-huggin' third.

Then from five thousand throats and more there rose a lusty yell,
It rumbled through the valley; it rattled in the dell;
It knocked upon the mountain and recoiled upon the flat,
For Casey, mighty Casey, was advancing to the bat.

There was ease in Casey's manner as he stepped into his place;
There was pride in Casey's bearing and a smile on Casey's face,
And when, responding to the cheers, he lightly doffed his hat,
No stranger in the crowd could doubt 'twas Casey at the bat.

Ten thousand eyes were on him as he rubbed his hands with dirt;
Five thousand tongues applauded when he wiped them on his shirt.
Then, while the writhing pitcher ground the ball into his hip,
Defiance gleamed in Casey's eye, a sneer curled Casey's lip.

And now the leather-covered sphere came hurtling through the air,
And Casey stood a-watching it in haughty grandeur there,
Close by the sturdy batsman the ball unheeded sped.
"That ain't my style," said Casey. "Strike one," the umpire said.

From the benches, black with people, there went up a muffled roar,
Like the beating of the storm-waves on a stern and distant shore.
"Kill him; kill the umpire!" shouted someone from the stand—
And it's likely they'd have killed him had not Casey raised his hand.

With a smile of Christian charity great Casey's visage shone;
He stilled the rising tumult; he bade the game go on;
He signaled to the pitcher, and once more the spheroid flew;
But Casey still ignored it, and the umpire said, "Strike two."

"Fraud," cried the maddened thousands, and echo answered "Fraud,"
But one scornful look from Casey, and the multitude was awed.
They saw his face grow stern and cold; they saw his muscles strain,
And they knew that Casey wouldn't let that ball go by again.

The sneer is gone from Casey's lip; his teeth are clenched in hate;
He pounds with cruel violence his bat upon the plate.
And now the pitcher holds the ball, and now he lets it go,
And now the air is shattered by the force of Casey's blow.

Oh! somewhere in this favored land the sun is shining bright;
The band is playing somewhere, and somewhere hearts are light.
And somewhere men are laughing, and somewhere children shout;
But there is no joy in Mudville—mighty Casey has Struck Out. ❖

"Strike one" the Umpire Said

Illustration by Dan Sayre Groesbeck for *Casey at the Bat*, 1912.

Yankee Helmets, Yankee Stadium, New York City **by Danielle Weil, September 1983.**

Talk About Colorful Guys

from Lawrence S. Ritter's *The Glory of Their Times*

◆

DAVY JONES

I WAS PLAYING in the Big Leagues in 1901, when Mr. William McKinley was President, and baseball attracted all sorts of people in those days. We had stupid guys, smart guys, tough guys, mild guys, crazy guys, college men, slickers from the city, and hicks from the country. And back then a country kid was likely to *really* be a country kid. We'd call them hayseeds or rubes. Nowadays I don't think there's much difference between city kids and country kids. Anyway, nothing like there used to be. . . .

Talk about colorful guys, take Rube Waddell or Germany Schaefer. I doubt if fellows like that could exist in baseball today. Too rambunctious, you know. They'd upset the applecart.

I played with Germany Schaefer on the Chicago Cubs in 1902, and again on the Detroit Tigers later on. What a man! What stunts he could pull! I used to laugh at that guy till I cried. Far and away the funniest man I ever saw. He beat Charlie Chaplin any day in the week.

One day when I was on the Tigers—I think it was 1906, my first year with Detroit—we were in Chicago, playing the White Sox. Red Donahue

was pitching for us and Doc White, that great little left-hander, was pitching for the White Sox. We were behind, 2-1, going into the ninth inning. Then in the ninth we got a man on first base with two out, and the next man up was Donahue, who was easily one of the worst hitters in the league. So Bill Armour, who was managing Detroit then, looked up and down the bench and spotted Germany Schaefer sitting there— talking, as usual, to whoever would listen.

"How would you like to go up there and pinch-hit?" Bill asked him.

"Sure," he says, "I'd love to. I always could hit Doc White."

Meanwhile, Red Donahue is already getting all set in the batter's box. Red was an awful hitter, but there was nothing in the whole world he loved more than digging in at that plate and taking his cuts.

"Hey, Red," yells Schaefer, "the manager wants me to hit for you."

"What?" Red roars. "Who the hell are you to hit for me?" And he slams his bat down and comes back and sits way down at the end of the bench, with his arms folded across his chest. Madder than a wet hen.

Well, Schaefer walked out there and just as he was about to step into the batter's box he stopped, took off his cap, and faced the grandstand.

"Ladies and gentlemen," he announced, "you are now looking at Herman Schaefer, better known as Herman the Great, acknowledged by one and all to be the greatest pinch hitter in the world. I am now going to hit the ball into the left-field bleachers. Thank you."

Then he turned around and stepped into the batter's box. Of course, everybody's giving him the old raspberry, because he never hit over two or three home runs in his life. But by golly, on the second ball Doc White pitched he did just exactly what he said he would: he hit it right smack into the left-field bleachers.

Boy oh boy, you should have seen him. He stood at that plate until the ball cleared the fence, and then he jumped straight up in the air, tore down to first base as fast as his legs would carry him, and proceeded to slide headfirst into the bag. After that he jumped up, yelled "Schaefer leads at the Quarter!" and started for second.

He slid into second—yelled "Schaefer leads at the Half!"—and continued the same way into third and then home. After he slid into home he stood up and announced: "Schaefer wins by a nose!" Then he brushed himself off, took off his cap, and walked over to the grandstand again.

"Ladies and gentlemen," he said, "I thank you for your kind attention."

Back on the bench everybody was laughing so hard they were falling all over themselves. Everybody except Red Donahue. He's still sitting there at the end of the bench with his arms folded, like a stone image, without the slightest expression of any kind on his face. . . .

It was during those years, I think about 1908, that I saw Germany Schaefer steal first base. Yes, *first* base. They say it can't be done, but I saw him do it. In fact, I was standing right on third

base, with my eyes popping out, when he did it.

We were playing Cleveland and the score was tied in a late inning. I was on third base, Schaefer on first, and Crawford was at bat. Before the pitcher wound up, Schaefer flashed me the sign for the double steal—meaning he'd take off for second on the next pitch, and when the catcher threw the ball to second I'd take off for home. Well, the pitcher wound up and pitched, and sure enough Schaefer stole second. But I had to stay right where I was, on third, because . . . the Cleveland catcher just held on to the ball. He refused to throw to second, knowing I'd probably make it home if he did.

So now we had men on second and third. Well, on the next pitch Schaefer yelled, "Let's try it again!" And with a blood-curdling shout he took off . . . *back to first base*, and dove in headfirst in a cloud of dust. He figured the catcher might throw to first—since he evidently wouldn't throw to second—and then I could come home same as before.

But nothing happened. Nothing at all. Everybody just stood there and watched Schaefer, with their mouths open, not knowing what the devil was going on. Me, too. Even if the catcher *had* thrown to first, I was too stunned to move, I'll tell you that. But the catcher didn't throw. He just stared! In fact, George Stovall, the Cleveland first baseman, was playing way back and didn't even come in to cover the bag. He just watched this madman running the wrong way on the base path and didn't know *what* to do.

The umpires were just as confused as everybody else. However, it turned out that at that time there wasn't any rule against a guy going from second back to first, if that's the way he wanted to play baseball, so they had to let it stand.

So there we were, back where we started, with Schaefer on first and me on third. And on the next pitch darned if he didn't let out another war whoop and take off *again* for second base. By this time the Cleveland catcher evidently had enough, because he finally threw

200

Balls in Bag, Memorial Stadium, Baltimore by **Danielle Weil, August 1990.**

to second to get Schaefer, and when he did I took off for home and *both* of us were safe. . . .

[That] story of Germany Schaefer running from second to first reminds me of another incident that happened when I was with the Chicago Cubs in 1902. We had a young pitcher on that club named Jimmy St. Vrain. He was a left-handed pitcher and a right-handed batter. But an absolutely terrible hitter—never even got a loud foul off anybody.

Well, one day we were playing the Pittsburgh Pirates and Jimmy was pitching for us. The first two times he went up to bat that day he looked simply awful. So when he came back after striking out the second time Frank Selee, our manager, said, "Jimmy, you're a left-handed pitcher, why don't you turn around and bat from the left side, too? Why not try it?"

Actually, Frank was half kidding, but Jimmy took him seriously. So the next time he went up he batted left-handed. Turned around and stood on the opposite side of the plate from where he was used to, you know. And darned if he didn't actually hit the ball. He tapped a slow roller down to Honus Wagner at shortstop and took off as fast as he could go . . . but instead of running to first base, he headed for *third!*

Oh, my God! What bedlam! Everybody yelling and screaming at poor Jimmy as he raced to third base, head down, spikes flying, determined to get there ahead of the throw. Later on, Honus told us that as a matter of fact he almost *did* throw the ball to third.

"I'm standing there with the ball in my hand," Honus said, "looking at this guy running from home to third, and for an instant there I swear I didn't know *where* to throw the damn ball. And when I finally did throw to first, I wasn't at all sure it was the right thing to do!" ❖

Chapter VII
GLORY

ALTHOUGH BASEBALL IS FULL of valuable lessons about disappointment, the real glory comes in victory. Reporting on a 1947 World Series game that ended suddenly—exactly how a World Series game should end—Red Smith wrote: "The game has been over for half an hour now, and still a knot of worshipers stand clustered, as around a shrine, out in right field adoring the spot on the wall which Cookie Lavagetto's line drive smote." Those are moments for which we ache.

The list of dazzling moments is as long and as subject to dispute as All-Star balloting: Reggie Jackson's five home runs in the 1977 World Series; Willie Mays's sprinting catch and whirling throw; Jackie Robinson stealing home; Hank Aaron's 715th homer. Some of them are captured in the pieces that follow: Bobby Thompson's line-drive homer, reimagined by novelist Don DeLillo; the race between Sammy Sosa and Mark McGwire to break Roger Maris's single-season home run record, recalled here by poet Quincy Troupe.

Sometimes the victory is personal; sometimes it's a team effort. In every case, it is precisely because this game is maddeningly difficult—that a batter who fails seven times out of ten is a star—that the clutch hit or diving catch can drive us mad with joy.

The moments we live for

Batter 1
by Charles Hobson, 1989.

204

"It's a great day
for a ballgame.
Let's play two."

—ERNIE BANKS

Three Base Hit by James H. Daugherty, 1914. Whitney Museum of American Art.

AMES DAUGHERTY

From
Underworld
◆
DON DeLILLO

BRANCA TAKES THE LAST of his warm-up tosses, flicking the glove to indicate a curve. Never mind the details of manner or appearance, the weight-bearing body at rest. Out on the mound he is strong and loose, cutting smoothly out of his windup, a man who wants the ball.

Furillo watching from right field. The stone-cut profile.

The bushy-haired man still pacing in the bleachers, moaning and shaking his head—call the men in the white suits and get him outta here. Talking to himself, head-wagging like a street-corner zealot with news of some distant affliction dragging ever closer. Siddown, shaddap, they tell him.

Frank keeps putting pages in Gleason's face.

He tells him, "Eat up, pal. Paper clears the palate."

When in steps Thomson.

The tall fleet Scot. Reminding himself as he gets set in the box. See the ball. Wait for the ball.

Russ is clutching the mike. Warm water and salt. Gargle, said his mother.

Thomson's not sure he sees things clearly. His eyeballs are humming. There's a feeling in his body, he's digging in, settling into his stance, crowd noise packing the sky, and there's a feeling that he has lost the link to his surroundings. Alone in all this rowdy-dow. See the ball. Watch and wait. He is frankly a little fuddled is Bobby. It's like the first waking moment of the day and you don't know whose house you're in.

Russ says, "Bobby Thomson up there swinging."

Mays down on one knee in the on-deck circle half leaning on his cradled bat and watching Branca go into a full windup, push-pull click-click, thinking it's all on him if Thomson falls, the season riding on him, and the jingle plays in his head, it's the radio embrace of the air itself, the mosaic of the air, and it will turn itself off when it's ready.

There's an emergency station under the stands and what the stadium cop has to do is figure out a way to get the stricken man down there without being overrun by a rampant stomping crowd. The victim looks okay considering. He is sitting down, waiting for the attendant to arrive with the wheelchair. All right, maybe he doesn't look so good. He looks pale, sick, worried and infarcted. But he can make a fist and stick out his tongue and there's not much the cop can do until the wheelchair arrives, so he might as well stand in the aisle and watch the end of the game.

Thomson in his bent stance, chin tucked, waiting.

Russ says, "One out, last of the ninth."

He says, "Branca pitches, Thomson takes a strike called on the inside corner."

He lays a heavy decibel on the word *strike*. He pauses to let the crowd reaction build. Do not talk against the crowd. Let the drama come from them.

Those big rich pages airing down from the upper deck.

Lockman stands near second and tries to wish a hit onto Thomson's bat. That may have been the pitch he wanted. Belt-high, a shade inside—won't see one that good again.

Russ says, "Bobby hitting at two ninety-two. He's had a single and a double and he drove in the Giants' first run with a long fly to center."

Lockman looks across the diamond at home. The double he hit is still a presence in his chest, it's chugging away in there, a body-memory that plays the moment over. He is peering into the deltoid opening between the catcher's knees. He sees the fingers dip, the blunt hand make a flapping action up and left. They'll give him the fastball high and tight and come back with the curve away. A pretty two-part scheme. Seems easy and sweet from here.

Russ says, "Brooklyn leads it four to two."

He says, "Runner down the line at third. Not taking any chances."

Thomson thinking it's all happening too fast. Thinking quick hands, see the ball, give yourself a chance.

Russ says, "Lockman without too big of a lead at second but he'll be running like the wind if Thomson hits one."

In the box seats J. Edgar Hoover plucks a magazine page off his shoulder, where the thing has lighted and stuck. At first he's annoyed that the object has come in contact with his body. Then his eyes fall upon the page. It is a color reproduction of a painting crowded with medieval figures who are dying or dead—a landscape of visionary havoc and ruin. Edgar has never seen a painting quite like this. It covers the page completely and must surely dominate the magazine. Across the red-brown earth, skeleton armies on the march. Men impaled on lances, hung from gibbets, drawn on spoked wheels fixed to the tops of bare trees, bodies open to the crows. Legions of the dead forming up behind shields made of coffin lids. Death himself astride a slat-ribbed hack, he is peaked for blood, his scythe held ready as he presses people in haunted swarms toward the entrance of some helltrap, an oddly modern construction that could be a subway tunnel or office corridor. A background of ash skies and burning ships. It is clear to Edgar that the page is from *Life* and he tries to work up an anger, he asks himself why a magazine called *Life* would want to reproduce a painting of such lurid and dreadful dimensions. But he can't take his eyes off the page.

Russ Hodges says, "Branca throws."

Gleason makes a noise that is halfway between a sigh and a moan. It is probably a sough, as of rustling surf in some palmy place. Edgar recalls the earlier blowout, Jackie's minor choking fit. He sees a deeper engagement here. He goes out into the aisle and up two steps, separating himself from the imminent discharge of animal, vegetable and mineral matter.

Not a good pitch to hit, up and in, but Thomson swings and tomahawks the ball and everybody, everybody watches. Except for Gleason who is bent over in his seat, hands locked behind his neck, a creamy strand of slime swinging from his lips.

Russ says, "There's a long drive."

His voice has a burst in it, a charge of expectation.

He says, "It's gonna be."

There's a pause all around him. Pafko racing toward the left-field corner.

He says, "I believe."

Pafko at the wall. Then he's looking up. People thinking where's the ball. The scant delay, the stay in time that lasts a hairsbreadth. And Cotter standing in section 35 watching the ball come in his direction. He feels his body turn to smoke. He loses sight of the ball when it climbs above the overhang and he thinks it will land in the upper deck. But before he can smile or shout or bash his neighbor on the arm. Before the moment can overwhelm him, the ball appears again, stitches visibly spinning, that's how near it hits, banging at an angle off a pillar—hands flashing everywhere.

Russ feels the crowd around him, a shudder passing through the stands, and then he is shouting into the mike and there is a surge of color and motion, a crash that occurs upward, stadium-wide, hands and faces and shirts, bands of rippling men, and he is outright shouting, his

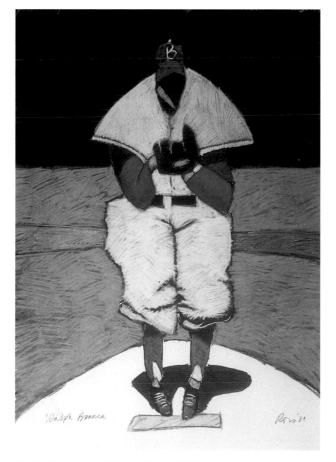

Ralph Branca by Thom Ross, 1989.

voice has a power he'd thought long gone—it may lift the top of his head like a cartoon rocket.

He says, "*The Giants win the pennant.*"

A topspin line drive. He tomahawked the pitch and the ball had topspin and dipped into the lower deck and there is Pafko at the 315 sign looking straight up with his right arm braced at the wall and a spate of paper coming down.

He says, "*The Giants win the pennant.*"

Yes, the voice is excessive with a little tickle of hysteria in the upper register. But it is mainly wham and whomp. He sees Thomson capering around first. The hat of the first-base coach—the first-base coach has flung his hat straight up. He went for a chin-high pitch and cold-cocked it good. The ball started up high and then sank, missing the facade of the upper deck and dipping into the seats below—pulled in, swallowed up—and the Dodger players stand looking, already separated from the event, staring flat into the shadows between the decks.

He says, "*The Giants win the pennant.*"

The crew is whooping. They are answering the roof bangers by beating on the walls and ceiling of the booth. People climbing the dugout roofs and the crowd shaking in its own noise. Branca on the mound in his tormented slouch. He came with a fastball up, a pitch that's tailing in, and the guy's supposed to take it for a ball. Russ is shouting himself right out of his sore throat, out of every malady and pathology and complaint and all the pangs of growing up and every memory that is not tender.

He says, "*The Giants win the pennant.*"

Four times. Branca turns and picks up the rosin bag and throws it down, heading toward the clubhouse now, his shoulders aligned at a slant—he begins the long dead trudge. Paper falling everywhere. Russ knows he ought to settle down and let the mike pick up the sound of the swelling bedlam around him. But he can't stop shouting, there's nothing left of him but shout.

He says, "Bobby Thomson hits into the lower deck of the left-field stands."

He says, "The Giants win the pennant and they're going crazy.

He says, "They're going crazy."

Then he raises a pure shout, wordless, a holler from the old days—it is fiddlin' time, it is mountain music on WCKY at five-thirty in the morning. The thing comes jumping right out of him, a jubilation, it might be *heyyy-ho* or it might be *oh-boyyy* shouted backwards or it might be something else entirely—hard to tell when they don't use words. And Thomson's teammates gathering at home plate and Thomson circling the bases in gamesome leaps, buckjumping—he is forever Bobby now, a romping boy lost to time, and his breath comes so fast he doesn't know if he can handle all the air that's pouring in. He sees men in a helter-skelter line waiting at the plate to pummel him—his teammates, no better fellows in the world, and there's a look in their faces, they are stunned by a happiness that has collapsed on them, bright-eyed under their caps. ❖

210

[OPPOSITE]
Saturday Afternoon at Sportman's Park
by Edward Laning, 1944.

GLORY

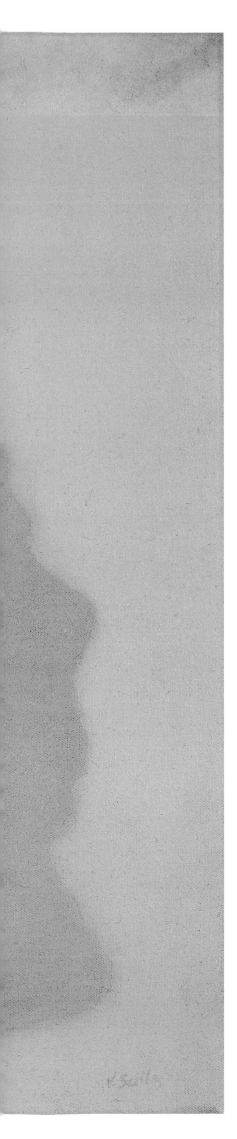

Albuquerque
by Vincent Scilla, 1988.

[FOLLOWING PAGES]
Sandy Amoros
by Andy Jurinko, 1996.

213

In Case You Thought
They Played for Money

◆

ROBERT FINK

Next Saturday catch Baseball's
Game of the Week. Study
the man in right, the forgotten one
who dreams of left-handed teams,
all pull hitters who send him deep
to make the leaping snag,
glove always just above the wall.
Young women smile behind their hands.
The Commissioner's mother phones
to say an apple pie is cooling on the sill,
she's set an extra place for dinner.

From
Swinging for Glory

◆

QUINCY TROUPE

    it was a chase of two men, neither perfect, in each other's
corner, back to back,
    after all is said & done, one black, one white, in a country
divided by chance,
    birth, most found themselves cheering both, over a final, stormy
weekend,

    it was beautiful, for one baseball season, two men
linked themselves back,
    with honor to babe ruth & roger maris's towering home run balls,
with a chance
    both would stand together, as one, over one last, glorious,
stormy weekend

Baseball by Andy Warhol, 1962.
© 2000 Andy Warhol Foundation for the Visual Arts. New York/ARS, New York

[OPPOSITE]
Willie Mays
by Mike Schacht, 1989.

Baseball Canto

LAWRENCE FERLINGHETTI

Watching baseball
sitting in the sun
eating popcorn
reading Ezra Pound

and wishing Juan Marichal
would hit a hole right through
the Anglo-Saxon tradition
in the First Canto
and demolish the barbarian invaders

When the San Francisco Giants take the field
and everybody stands up to the National Anthem
with some Irish tenor's voice
piped over the loudspeakers
with all the players struck dead in their places
and the white umpires like Irish cops
in their black suits and little black caps
pressed over their hearts
standing straight and still
like at some funeral of a blarney bartender
and all facing East
as if expecting some Great White Hope
or the Founding Fathers
to appear on the horizon
like 1066 or 1776 or all that

But Willie Mays appears instead
in the bottom of the first
and a roar goes up
   as he clouts the first one into the sun
    and takes off
     like a footrunner from Thebes

   The ball is lost in the sun
    and maidens wail after him
     but he keeps running
      through the Anglo-Saxon epic

And Tito Fuentes comes up
  looking like a bullfighter
  in his tight pants and small pointed shoes

 And the rightfield bleachers go mad
   with chicanos & blacks & Brooklyn beerdrinkers
    "Sweet Tito! Sock it to heem, Sweet Tito!"
And Sweet Tito puts his foot in the bucket
   and smacks one that don't come back at all
   and flees around the bases
  like he's escaping from the United Fruit Company
   as the gringo dollar beats out the Pound
    and Sweet Tito beats it out
    like he's beating out usury
    not to mention fascism and anti-semitism

And Juan Marichal comes up
 and the chicano bleachers go loco again
  as Juan belts the first fast ball
   out of sight
    and rounds first and keeps going
  and rounds second and rounds third
     and keeps going
    and hits pay-dirt
  to the roars of the grungy populace
As some nut presses the backstage panic button
for the tape-recorded National Anthem again
to save the situation

but it don't stop nobody this time
in their revolution round the loaded white bases
in this last of the great Anglo-Saxon epics
in the *Territorio Libre* of baseball

*Looking for a Curveball
in Cuernavaca*
by Karl Wirsum, 1983.

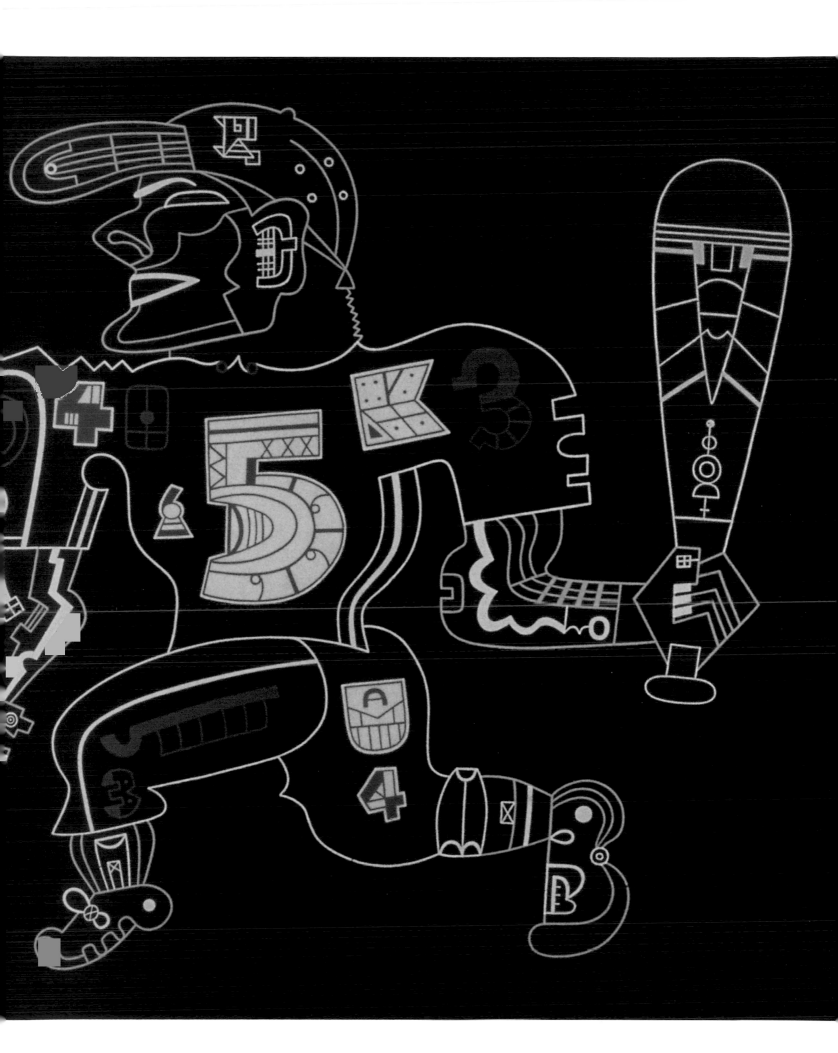

From the Shadows
by John Dobbs, 1993–96.

Turning Pro

◆

ISHMAEL REED

There are just so many years
you can play amateur baseball
without turning pro
All of a sudden you realize
you're ten years older than
everybody in the dugout
and that the shortstop could
be your son

The front office complains
about your slowness in making
the lineup
They send down memos about
your faulty bunts and point out
how the runners are always faking
you out
"His ability to steal bases
has faded" they say
They say they can't convince
the accountant that there's such
a thing as "Old Time's Sake"

But just as the scribes were
beginning to write you
off
as a has-been on his last leg
You pulled out that fateful
shut-out
and the whistles went off
and the fireworks scorched a
747
And your name lit up the scoreboard
and the fans carried you on their
shoulders right out of the stadium
and into the majors

To Satch

◆

SAMUEL ALLEN

Sometimes I feel like I will *never* stop

Just go on forever

Till one fine mornin'

I'm gonna reach up and grab me a handfulla stars

Swing out my long lean leg

And whip three hot strikes burnin' down the heavens

And look over at God and say,

How about that!

Satchel Paige by George Strock, June 1, 1941.

The YOUTH'S COMPANION *April* 1935
combined with
American Boy 10¢
Founded 1827

"Good-by, Babe Ruth!"
by
H. G. SALSINGER

Game Called

◆

GRANTLAND RICE

[*Rice, "the Dean of American Sports Writers," wrote this piece on August 14, 1948, the day Babe Ruth died.*]

Game called by darkness—let the curtain fall,
No more remembered thunder sweeps the field.
No more the ancient echoes hear the call
To one who wore so well both sword and shield.
The Big Guy's left us with the night to face,
And there is no one who can take his place.

Game called—and silence settles on the plain.
Where is the crash of ash against the sphere?
Where is the mighty music, the refrain
That once brought joy to every waiting ear?
The Big Guy's left us, lonely in the dark,
Forever waiting for the flaming spark.

Game called—what more is there for one to say?
How dull and drab the field looks to the eye.
For one who ruled it in a golden day
Has waved his cap to bid us all good-by.
The Big Guy's gone—by land or sky or foam
May the Great Umpire call him "safe at home."

[OPPOSITE]
American Boy cover, April 1935.

From
The Natural

◆

BERNARD MALAMUD

THE UMPIRE ROARED in for a batter to come out, and after a while, as the players fidgeted and Pop fumed, Roy sighed and picked up Wonderboy. He slowly walked up the steps.

"Knock the cover off of it," Pop yelled.

"Attention, please," the P.A. man announced. "Roy Hobbs, number forty-five, batting for Baily."

A groan rose from the stands and turned into a roar of protest.

Otto Zipp jumped up and down on his seat, shaking his furious little fist at home plate.

"Throw him to the dogs," he shouted, and filled the air with his piercing curses.

Glancing at the wives' box, Roy saw that Memo had her head turned away. He set his jaw and advanced to the plate. His impulse was to knock the dirt out of his cleats but he refrained because he did not want to harm his bat in any way. Waiting for the pitcher to get set, Roy wiped his palms on his pants and twitched his cap. He lifted Wonderboy and waited rocklike for the throw.

He couldn't tell the color of the pitch that came at him. All he could think of was that he was sick to death of waiting, and tongue-out thirsty to begin. The ball was now a dew drop staring him in the eye so he stepped back and swung from the toes.

Wonderboy flashed in the sun. It caught the sphere where it was biggest. A noise like a twenty-one gun salute cracked the sky. There was a straining, ripping sound and a few drops of rain spattered to the ground. The ball screamed toward the pitcher and seemed suddenly to dive down at his feet. He grabbed it to throw to first and realized to his horror that he held only the cover. The rest of it, unraveling cotton thread as it rode, was headed into the outfield.

Roy was rounding first when the ball plummeted like a dead bird into center field; Attempting to retrieve and throw, the Philly fielder got tangled in thread. The second baseman rushed up, bit the cord and heaved the ball to the catcher but Roy had passed third and made home, standing. The umpire called him safe and immediately a rhubarb boiled. The Phils' manager and his players charged out of the dugout and were joined by the nine men on the field. At the same time, Pop, shouting in defense of the ump, rushed forth with all the Knights but Bump. The umpire, caught between both teams, had a troublesome time of it and was shoved this way and that. He tossed out two men on each side but by then came to the decision that the hit was a ground rules double. Flores had scored and the game was tied up. Roy was ordered back to second, and Pop announced he was finishing the game under protest. Somebody then shouted it was raining cats and dogs. The stands emptied like a yawn and the players piled into the dugouts. By the time Roy got in from second he was wading in water ankle deep. Pop sent him into the clubhouse for a change of uniform but he could have saved himself the trouble because it rained steadily for three days. The game was recorded as a 2-2 tie, to be replayed later in the season.

In the locker room Pop asked Roy to explain why he thought the cover had come off the ball.

"That's what you said to do, wasn't it?"

"That's right," said Pop, scratching his bean.

The next day he told Roy he was withdrawing his release and would hereafter use him as a pinch hitter and substitute fielder. ❖

[OPPOSITE]
Leonardo Series:
YES/umpire 1
by Charles Hobson, 1990.

[FOLLOWING PAGES]
The Wide Swing
by Harvey Dinnerstein, 1974.

Y E S

YES/umpire 1   C. Hobson

GLORY

With Courage and with Grace

◆

GEORGE ELLARD

[*Ellard was a member of the undefeated
1869 Cincinnati Red Stockings.*]

We used no mattress on our hands,
No cage upon our face;
We stood right up and caught the ball
With courage and with grace.

[ABOVE]
Home Run Cigar label, ca. 1880.

[OPPOSITE]
**Detail from *Baseball Players Practicing*
by Thomas Eakins, 1875.
Rhode Island School of Design, Museum of Art.**

Time-Life Books is a division of Time Life Inc.
Time-Life is a trademark of Time Warner Inc. and affiliated companies.

TIME LIFE INC.
Chairman and Chief Executive Officer: Jim Nelson
President and Chief Operating Officer: Steven Janas
Senior Executive Vice President and Chief Operating Officer: Mary Davis Holt
Senior Vice President and Chief Financial Officer: Christopher Hearing

TIME-LIFE BOOKS
President: Larry Jellen
Senior Vice President, New Markets: Bridget Boel
Vice President, Home and Hearth Markets: Nicholas M. DiMarco
Vice President, Content Development: Jennifer L. Pearce

TIME-LIFE TRADE PUBLISHING
Vice President and Publisher: Neil S. Levin
Senior Sales Director: Richard J. Vreeland
Director, Marketing and Publicity: Inger Forland
Director of Trade Sales: Dana Hobson
Director of Custom Publishing: John Lalor
Director of Rights Licensing: Olga Vezeris

BASEBALL
New Product Development Manager: Lori A. Woehrle
Executive Editor: Robert Somerville
Director of Design: Tina Taylor
Project Manager: Jennifer L. Ward
Director of Production: Carolyn Bounds

PRODUCED BY FAIR STREET PRODUCTIONS AND WELCOME ENTERPRISES, INC.
Project Directors: Deborah Bull, Lena Tabori
Project Editor: Deborah Bull
Project Manager: Natasha Tabori Fried
Art Director: Gregory Wakabayashi
Photo Researcher: Deborah Anderson/Photosearch, Inc.
Traffic Coordinator: Shaie Dively/Photosearch, Inc.

Compilation copyright © 2001 by Fair Street Productions and Welcome Enterprises, Inc.

School and library distribution by Time-Life Education, P.O. Box 85026, Richmond, Virginia 23285-5026.

Library of Congress Cataloging-in-Publication Data
Baseball : the national pastime in art and literature / edited by David Colbert.
    p.   cm.
    ISBN 0-7370-0102-X (hardcover)
1. Baseball—Literary collections. 2. American literature. 3. Baseball in art. 4. Baseball.
I. Colbert, David.
PS509.B37 B38 2001
810.8'0355—dc21   00—51183

Printed in Singapore
10 9 8 7 6 5 4 3 2 1

Literary Credits

Art Credits

Archives and Records Center
PAGES 59–65: Transcendental Graphics
PAGE 66: Claes Oldenburg, *Standing Mitt with Ball*, 1973. Lithograph in four colors, 19 1/2 x 21 3/8 in. (49.5 x 54.3 cm). Published by Landfall Press, Chicago. Courtesy of Claes Oldenburg and Coosje van Bruggen
PAGE 68: © Jon Lezinsky at Scott Hull Associates, www.scotthull.com
PAGE 71: © Mike Schacht
PAGE 72: © Jon Lezinsky at Scott Hull Associates, www.scotthull.com
PAGE 74: National Baseball Hall of Fame Library, Cooperstown, NY
PAGE 77: © Robert Valdes, NY
PAGES 78, 82–83: © John Hull. Originally published in *John Hull: Paintings & Drawings of the Louisville Redbirds*, The J. B. Speed Art Museum
PAGE 85: Permission for the reproduction of paintings by Gerald Garston is granted by Lois F. Garston and the estate of Gerald Garston
PAGE 86: © Charles Hobson, San Francisco. www.charleshobson.com
PAGES 88–89: Collection of Howard University Gallery of Art, Washington, D.C. Courtesy Jacob and Gwendolyn Lawrence Foundation, Boston
PAGES 92–93: National Baseball Hall of Fame Library, Cooperstown, NY
PAGES 96–97: The Gladstone Collection of Baseball Art
PAGE 99: Printed by permission of the Norman Rockwell Family Trust. © 2000 The Norman Rockwell Family Trust. The National Baseball Hall of Fame, Cooperstown, NY
PAGE 100: © Kelly LaDuke. *All Stars: One Team, One Season,* published by Longstreet Press, Inc.
PAGES 102–103: © Charles Hobson, San Francisco. www.charleshobson.com
PAGES 104–105: Courtesy Bill Goff, Inc.
PAGE 107: © Jon Lezinsky at Scott Hull Associates, www.scotthull.com
PAGE 108: National Baseball Hall of Fame Library, Cooperstown, NY
PAGE 111: The Gladstone Collection of Baseball Art
PAGE 112: National Baseball Hall of Fame Library, Cooperstown, NY
PAGE 116: Transcendental Graphics
PAGES 118–119: Marjoric Phillips, *Night Baseball*, 1951. Oil on canvas. 24 1/4 x 36 in. Gift of the artist 1951 or 1952. © The Phillips Collection, Washington, D.C.
PAGE 121: © Steven Skollar, Private Collection
PAGES 122, 127: Courtesy Bill Goff, Inc.
PAGE 128: © 2001 Jeffrey Rubin. www.jeffreyrubin.com
PAGE 130: © Stephen Fox. O.K. Harris Works of Art, NY
PAGE 133: Charles M. Conlon/The Sporting News
PAGE 134: © Thom Ross, Ravenswork Studio, Seattle, Washington. Private Collection
PAGE 136: National Baseball Hall of Fame Library, Cooperstown, NY
PAGES 138–139: © Ralph Fasanella, ACA Galleries, New York
PAGE 140: Transcendental Graphics
PAGES 142–143: © Jim Dow. Courtesy Janet Borden Gallery, New York
PAGE 145: © John Dobbs. ACA Galleries, New York
PAGES 146–147: © Andrew Radcliffe
PAGE 149: Transcendental Graphics
PAGE 151: Permission for the reproduction of paintings by Gerald Garston is granted by Lois F. Garston and the estate of Gerald Garston
PAGE 152: Smithsonian American Art Museum, Washington, D.C./Art Resource, New York
PAGE 155: © Charles Hobson, San Francisco. www.charleshobson.com
PAGE 156: © John Hull. Courtesy: McKinsey and Co., New York, NY. Photo by Sarah Wells

PAGES 158-159: Nelson Rosenberg, *Out at Third,* undated. Watercolor and gouache on paper. 15 x 21 7/8 in. © The Phillips Collection, Washington, DC
PAGE 160: Transcendental Graphics
PAGE 162: *Saturday Evening Post,* September 2, 1950. © 1950 SEPS: Curtis Publishing Co., Agent
PAGE 164: © Pamela Patrick
PAGE 167: The Gladstone Collection of Baseball Art
PAGES 168–169: Ferdinand Warren, *Night Ball Game*, 1946. Oil on canvas, 32 x 47 inches. Georgia Museum of Art, University of Georgia; Eva Underhill Holbrook Memorial Collection of American Art, Gift of Alfred H. Holbrook. GMOA 47.174
PAGE 170: © Lance Richbourg. Courtesy of O.K. Harris Gallery, NY
PAGES 172–173: © Christie's Images, NY
PAGES 174–175: © 2001 Jeffrey Rubin. www.jeffreyrubin.com
PAGE 177: Peter de Sève, New York
PAGE 178: © Arnold Roth
PAGE 180: © 2000 Red Grooms/Artists Rights Society (ARS), New York
PAGE 183: Christie's Images, NY
PAGES 184–185: Transcendental Graphics
PAGES 186–187: *Saturday Evening Post,* March 20, 1957. © 1957 SEPS: Curtis Publishing Co., Agent
PAGE 188, 191: Transcendental Graphics. Courtesy of the Chicago National League Ball Club, Inc.
PAGES 192–193: © Vincent Scilla. Oil on canvas, 24 x 30 inches. Collection of Stephen Milman
PAGES 194, 197: Mary Evans Picture Library
PAGES 198, 201: © Danielle Weil
PAGE 202: © Charles Hobson, San Francisco. www.charleshobson.com
PAGE 205: © Arthur K. Miller. Courtesy O.K. Harris Gallery, NY
PAGES 206–207: James H. Daugherty, *Three Base Hit*, 1914. Collection of Whitney Museum of American Art Purchase, 77.40. Photograph Copyright © 2000: Whitney Museum of American Art
PAGE 209: © Thom Ross, Ravenswork Studio, Seattle, Washington. Private Collection, Frank and Maureen Londy
PAGE 211: The Gladstone Collection of Baseball Art
PAGE 212: © Vincent Scilla. Collection of artist
PAGES 214–215: © Andy Jurinko, New York
PAGE 217: © The Andy Warhol Foundation, Inc./ARS/Art Resource, NY
PAGE 218: © Mike Schacht
PAGE 221: © Karl Wirsum. Photo courtesy Phyllis Kind Gallery, New York
PAGES 222–223: © John Dobbs. ACA Galleries, New York;
PAGE 225: George Strock/TimePix
PAGE 226: *American Boy,* April 1935. Private Collection
PAGE 228: © Lance Richbourg, 1994. Courtesy Superstock
PAGE 231: © Charles Hobson, San Francisco. www.charleshobson.com
PAGES 232–233: © Harvey Dinnerstein. Collection of Capricorn Galleries, Potomac, Maryland
PAGE 234: Thomas Eakins, *Baseball Players Practicing*, 1875. Museum of Art, Rhode Island School of Design; Jesse Metcalf and Walter H. Kimball Funds. Photo by Cathy Carver
PAGE 235: Transcendental Graphics
PAGE 240: National Baseball Hall of Fame Library, Cooperstown, NY

THE EDITORS GRATEFULLY ACKNOWLEDGE THE HELP OF THE VARIOUS INSTITUTIONS AND INDIVIDUALS WHO SUPPLIED ART AND TEXT FOR THIS BOOK.

Every attempt has been made to obtain permission to reproduce materials protected by copyright. Where omissions may have occurred, the producers will be happy to acknowledge this in future printings.

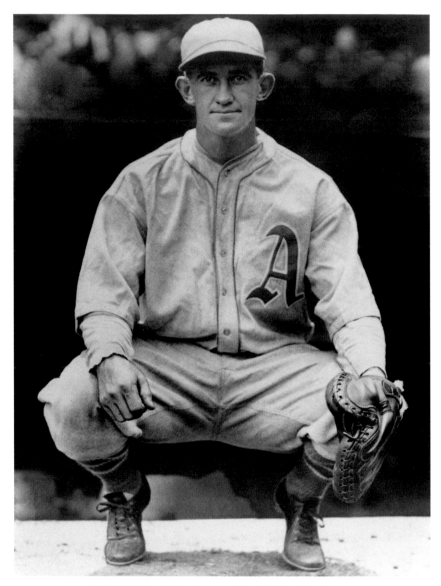

Philadelphia Athletics catcher Mickey Cochrane
by W. C. Greene, ca. 1929.

ACKNOWLEDGMENTS

THOUGH BY PUBLISHING CUSTOM the editor is named on the title page, this book truly was conceived and created by a team on which I was only one player. Pencil these names on your scorecard: Deborah Bull (player-manager) and Deborah Anderson at Fair Street Productions; Gregory Wakabayashi, Natasha Tabori Fried, and Lena Tabori at Welcome Enterprises; and Jennifer Ward, Tina Taylor, and Bob Somerville at Time Life. (For those readers who counted, no, we did not narrow the group to nine on purpose.) Also, for his clutch ninth-inning advice I wish to thank Miles Kronby, who delivers both keen literary judgment and a terrifying curveball. —DC